CONTENTS

ABOUT THE AUTHOR

Sandy Green qualified as a nursery nurse in the early 1970s. She has a broad knowledge and experience of early years education and care. In the late 1980s she entered teaching, and developed a particular interest in research. She is currently course coordinator for both the BTEC National Diploma in Early Years and the CACHE Advanced Diploma in Childcare and Education (ADCE) at Norton Radstock College.

ACKNOWLEDGEMENTS

Thanks are due to my family for their patience and encouragement, and to colleagues for their continued interest and support. Particular thanks go to my daughter Hannah and to Jayne Olpin, who have both spent many hours reading and commenting on the book during its development.

The photographs of children at play, and of nursery nursing students on the BTEC National Diploma in Childhood Studies course were taken with kind permission of Norton Radstock College and also the staff and parents of children in the college crèche.

The author and publishers would like to thank the following people and organisations for permission to reproduce material:

The *Guardian*, NCH Action for Children, Christine Hobart and Jill Frankel, Christine Jameson and Madeline Watson, Jayne Olpin.

Every effort has been made to contact copyright holders and we apologise if any have been overlooked.

PREFACE

My interest in research developed whilst studying for my M.Ed. at the University of the West of England. Many of the skills required and issues considered during the research process are relevant to both professional and private aspects of life.

Working with early years students on both the BTEC National Diploma in Childhood Studies and on the ADCE course, I have seen students' personal development blossom as they approach their research project or dissertation, succeeding in tasks and situations which they had not previously thought themselves capable of. For me this upholds the value of the personal research element within both academic and vocational courses.

However, research methodology texts can often seem wordy and off-putting, proving to be a barrier for some students. With this in mind I set out to write a user-friendly text which would be more accessible to the students I work with, and other students working in health and social care at a similar academic level.

INTRODUCTION

Research Methods in Health, Social and Early Years Care sets out the process of researching for an individual project. It will be particularly useful for first-time researchers, showing a clear pathway through the many actions that need to be taken and the points that need to be considered. The primary focus has been to aid the learning of research methodology for Level 3 students in care and early years, with direct relevance to programmes such as the Edexcel (BTEC) National Diploma in Early Years and the Advanced GNVQ in Health and Social Care, each with a specific research component. The straightforward approach used, together with the simple, clear English text may also help consolidate aspects of research for more experienced researchers.

A variety of books and journals are referred to as sources of material for the examples and case studies included. These cover both early years and adult care, reflecting the academic and research interests of students within the broad field of health, social care and early years.

Using this book

This book includes practical examples, activities and case studies to illustrate points and raise questions for the reader.

There are consistent features throughout the book. Each chapter begins with a list of the main points that are to be covered. Case studies are usually followed by questions to help consolidate the material. You will find checklists, examples, suggested activities and 'Remember' points throughout, consolidating what you have read and extending your thinking.

Some chapters include photocopiable pages which are designed to help with the practical task of carrying out a research project.

Each chapter of the book is a section in its own right, although each guides you to relevant aspects of other chapters for additional information. Chapter 8, 'Planning a small-scale study', brings aspects of each of the previous chapters together, guiding you through the planning of your own work.

Each chapter ends with a summary, restating some of the main points, and a list of the key terms introduced in the chapter. The glossary at the end of the book gives a brief explanation of all the key terms, which are in **bold** print at their first mention in the text.

The Appendices list some useful sources of information and relevant journals and magazines, and there is also a list of books and articles for further reading.

1 APPROACHES TO RESEARCH

> ## This chapter covers:
> - Why do we carry out research?
> - What is research?
> - First-time research
> - The purpose and role of research in health care

On a world-wide scale, the outcomes of research help to advance developments in areas such as science, health care and medicine. On an individual level, research can help us develop further our knowledge and understanding of an area of personal interest.

There are several different types of research. Each is valuable in appropriate circumstances, but most are not suitable for the length of project carried out by many first-time researchers (often referred to as small-scale projects). It is useful, however, for all researchers to have an outline understanding of the different approaches to research, and these will be briefly covered within this book.

Why do we carry out research?

Research can be approached in various ways depending on what the researcher is aiming to achieve. First-time researchers who are usually exploring a topic to develop their personal knowledge and understanding will rely mostly on **secondary data** (information collated and presented by someone else), putting their own slant onto a subject, and limiting **primary data** (information gathered by the researcher themselves) to a supportive role within their work. More experienced researchers put a greater focus on **primary research** methods (the methods used to gather their own data), supporting their findings from **secondary research** sources (the methods of obtaining secondary data). The research element of some courses specifies requirements regarding primary and secondary research, and students should read these carefully.

> ## Activity
> Think back over your lifetime, and perhaps that of your parents and grand-parents. What changes or new developments can you think of that have come about through research?

Clearly, advances such as heart surgery, cancer treatments and IVF (in-vitro fertilisation) have had a lasting impact on people's lives, and on society in general, and few of us will be involved in anything so life-changing. We can, however, acquire important new knowledge and experience for ourselves from carrying out research, which may offer us ideas for future careers, or encourage us to research further, beginning an increasing spiral of personal development.

What is research?

Research is the investigation of a topic for a purpose. This purpose may be to look at an area from a particular perspective, or to explore a particular theory. Methods of research vary considerably, and by understanding them you will be able to choose the method most suitable for your individual project. Methods of research can be divided into two main categories: primary research and secondary research. This chapter discusses both, and also explains the significant and commonly used terms **quantitative research** and **qualitative research**.

PRIMARY AND SECONDARY RESEARCH

The simplest way to explain the difference between primary and secondary research is to think of primary research as being an enquiry that you have carried out yourself (it need not be unique, but it must be your own). Secondary research is the use of material researched and/or written by others.

Although it is likely that you will use more secondary research than primary, you will find that a greater proportion of this chapter is given to explaining primary research methods. This is because the procedures for carrying out good primary research can be quite complex and it is important that you get your primary research right.

Examples of primary and secondary research methods

Primary	Secondary
Interviews	Literature searches
Questionnaires	Media analysis
Action research	Technology-based research
Observation	Case studies
Case studies	Statistical analysis

Chapter 2 gives a clear explanation of each of the above, using examples to illustrate.

QUANTITATIVE AND QUALITATIVE RESEARCH

Research can be either quantitative or qualitative, and sometimes a combination of both. The terms 'quantitative' and 'qualitative' are regularly used in research. They are most easily understood as follows.

Quantitative

Quantitative research produces results which can be expressed using numbers or statistics. This is useful if you are exploring the extent to which something happens, or if your focus is on 'How many ... ?' or 'How often ... ?' 'How many people think ... ?' or 'How often do people go ... ?' and so on.

Example

Following the Government's pledge to fund the education of all four-year-olds, David Anstey, a researcher for the local education authority (LEA) in New Town, asked 100 parents of young children in the local shopping centre which nursery or school they would choose to send their four-year-old to, setting out their choices. The outcome was measurable (and therefore quantitative) because it gave David the following statistics to work with.

Of the parents asked:

■ 5 would choose provision A
■ 16 would choose provision B
■ 44 would choose provision C
■ 10 would choose provision D
■ 2 would choose provision E
■ 23 would choose provision F.

As the researcher, David was able to make a clear comment on the outcomes, and show his findings on charts (Figures 1.1 and 1.2).

Qualitative

Qualitative research obtains viewpoints and personal feelings from its participants. These are not easily measured. In contrast to quantitative researchers, qualitative researchers wish to gain insight into their topic rather than make an analysis of

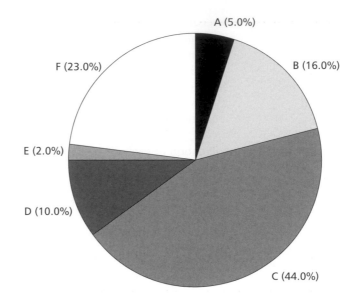

Figure 1.1   David's findings set out as a pie chart

statistics. They are less concerned with 'How many?' and more concerned with 'Why?' and 'What?'

In a survey such as the one described above, the emphasis would be on the reasons for the viewpoints of the parents rather than simply the choice of provision made by them for their children. The outcome would not be so easily measurable, but would be useful as a point of discussion.

Activity
What would you have asked if you were the researcher for the above subject, taking a qualitative approach? Make a note of your main questions.

Example
This example, like the first, focuses on research carried out with the shoppers in New Town, where Beverley Hall, a local early years student, asked 100 parents of young children what would influence their choice of education provision for their four-year-olds. The results of this gave Beverley a greater understanding of what was important to the parents of that particular community than did David's results (he simply found out that more parents would choose provision C, but not why), but Beverley's findings would not be easily transferred into graph form, and might have less impact if presented visually.

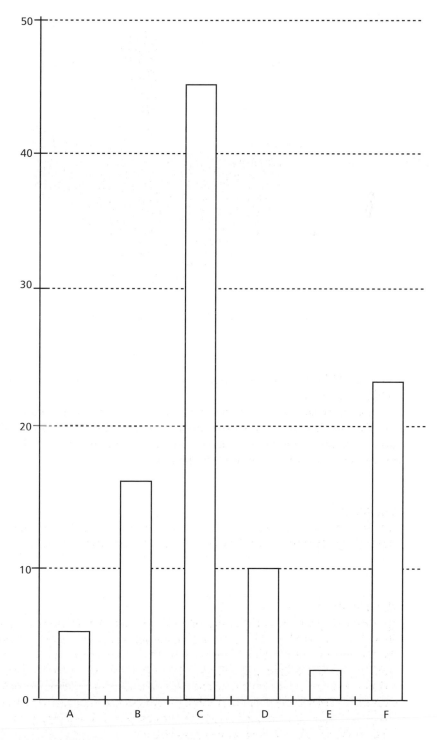

Figure 1.2   David's findings set out as a bar chart

The usefulness of the information you receive is directly linked to the questions you ask. It is important that your questions are well thought out. Chapter 2 discusses the techniques of writing questions.

Research can at times be both quantitative and qualitative. It may involve counting the opinions as well as identifying and evaluating those opinions. Your tutor will help you to clarify where your research falls if you are unsure.

METHODS OF RESEARCH

Set out below are a range of differing types of research, together with examples. They are:

- longitudinal research
- cross-sectional research
- cross-cultural research.

Longitudinal research
Longitudinal research is a study carried out over a considerable period of time. The researcher follows the progress of something or someone (for example, a child's development) rather than taking a 'snapshot' of what is happening at any one particular time.

Example

A good example is the regular filming and interviewing of a group of children over the last four decades, widely recognised by the title of the first televised programme, *7 Up* (Granada ITV). The series continued with *14 Up*, *21 Up*, and so on, following the children's lives every seven years, noting differences and similarities and discussing the influences upon the individuals involved.

Cross-sectional research
Cross-sectional research takes a 'slice' (a cross-section) of its **target group** and bases its overall findings on the views or behaviours of those targeted, assuming them to be typical of the whole group.

Example

An example of this would be interviewing one member of each generation of a family (considered typical for their culture or lifestyle) on a specific topic, with the researcher then taking the responses of the participants as valid for each member of a generation in a similar set of circumstances.

Cross-cultural research

When taking a **cross-cultural** approach, researchers apply the main focus of their research to a range of cultures, either within a single community or across a range of communities.

> ## Example
> If researchers were looking at the expectations made of children by different cultures, it would be found that in cultures such as the Gusii of Kenya:
>
> > there is greater emphasis on training in early life, mainly training for work and responsibility ...
> > *(Whiting and Whiting 1975, cited in Oates 1994, p. 11)*
>
> This clearly contrasts with the play-based childhood of most of the Western world.

First-time research

As a relatively new researcher you will not be expected to address any of the above three research types. You are most likely to be researching as part of a course of study. Your research will therefore be relevant to you as an individual and help you to build on your knowledge and understanding of a particular subject that you are interested in, or will be of help to you in the future. As stated in the introduction, this book will help steer you through the process of managing your project.

ISSUES OF OBJECTIVITY AND SUBJECTIVITY

In all forms of research it is important that research remains as objective as possible. This means being as careful as possible not to let your personal opinions, biases or prejudices influence what you are doing, or how you interpret your findings. There should be no indication of where your views lie. The research term for this is 'value free', and it relates to the experiences in your life which have influenced your views. At times the results of research are not what you as the researcher were expecting. It is important to accept the facts as they are, analyse the reasons and write up the report accurately. If as a researcher you allow preconceived ideas or personal views to influence the outcomes of your work it becomes subjective. Subjectivity is the opposite of objectivity in that personal bias and opinion is apparent. Subjective research outcomes are therefore of little value to anyone as there is no guarantee that the information gathered has not been influenced by (you) the researcher. Human nature makes pure objectivity almost impossible, but recognising and acknowledging our personal opinions and biases helps us, as researchers, to be as objective as we can.

FORMING A HYPOTHESIS, AN ISSUE OR A RESEARCH QUESTION

From the outset of your study you need to know what you are aiming to find out. This may result in the use of a research issue, a question or a **hypothesis**.

- An issue is a statement of fact or a concern that could be explored by the researcher.
- A question can be used when the researcher wishes to find out a specific answer.
- A hypothesis is a statement which the researcher sets out to either prove or disprove.

Setting a hypothesis forms a common part of a research **aim**. A hypothesis can take different forms and can be single ended or open ended. For example, 'Girls read more than boys' is single ended because it suggests which way the outcome is likely to be and can be proven right or wrong. Alternatively 'Stroking a pet affects stress levels' is an open ended hypothesis because it does not suggest a prediction, but simply infers that one factor will affect another. A research question or issue can sometimes give a clearer aim for you to work towards, but setting a hypothesis is often more interesting.

Activity

Consider the following examples of hypotheses. If you were the researcher how would you try to prove or disprove them? Which do you consider to be single ended and which open ended?

1 All women would stay at home with their babies for the first few years of their lives if they could afford to.
2 The more expensive residential homes provide better care than cheaper residential homes.
3 Multicultural play opportunities affect racial prejudice.
4 A greater range of play equipment has an effect on the quality of day nursery provision.
5 Training in communication improves staff interaction with residential clients.

Thinking these through will help you when you come to formulate your own overall aim for your study.

Activity

1 Refer once again to the hypothesis examples set out above. Turn each hypothesis into a research question.
2 Which 'style' works best for you? Why is that, do you think?

Once you have set yourself an issue, question or hypothesis to work towards you will move on to decide which research methods you will use.

The purpose and role of research in health care

The roles and responsibilities of health care staff move progressively from being purely occupational to being part of the health profession. Research plays a part in this. Reviews have been made of services offered and levels of practice carried out. Without the use of research there would be less information available to support the improvement of facilities, or to compare standards between different providers.

Activity

1   Consider your current (or a past) care placement or employment situation. This could be in early years, in adult care or in a health establishment.
    ■ How might it be affected by research? Think about who monitors its standards, quality and any changes.
    ■ What (if any) aspects do you know have already been directly influenced by research?
    ■ Can you think of ways in which it might have been indirectly affected?
2   Using relevant journals or magazines for the establishment being considered in the above activity, take time to review and analyse articles outlining research in that particular field of health or care.
    ■ What was the research about?
    ■ What was the rationale (the reason) behind it?
    ■ What research methods were used?
    ■ Have the outcomes of the research been justified?
    ■ What ethical issues can you identify within the research?

Chapter summary

■ Research has a purpose.
■ Research enables society to develop new ideas based on enquiry.
■ Research may involve a new line of enquiry (primary).
■ A previous piece of research may be referred to (secondary).
■ The results of research may be measurable (quantitative).
■ Research may simply give insight into a subject (qualitative).
■ Research can be used to compare, to explore theory or to identify change.
■ Research needs a specific focus, in the form of a hypothesis, an issue or a question.

KEY TERMS

You should now understand the following words and phrases. If you do not, go back through the chapter and review them.

Primary research   Qualitative research
Secondary research   Longitudinal research
Primary data   Cross-sectional research
Secondary data   Cross-cultural research
Quantitative research   Hypothesis

The following terms are dealt with more fully in Chapter 2:

Target group   Observation
Interview   Case study
Questionnaire   Statistics
Action research   Aim

2 METHODS OF RESEARCH

Choosing a method of research suitable for your own specific aims requires some experience and judgement, and you should seek guidance from your tutor before committing to any one approach.

This chapter outlines the key primary and secondary methods, remembering the following points:
- Primary methods focus on original research carried out by yourself.
- Secondary methods focus on drawing conclusions from research carried out by others.

Primary research methods

Primary research involves you, as the researcher, carrying out your own line of enquiry. This may have similarities to previous research carried out by another person, but as you involve different participants you are likely to obtain different results. Alternatively, your research may be a unique enquiry for your chosen topic.

Outlined on the following pages is a range of primary research methods, together with discussion covering:
- when and how to use them
- their advantages
- their disadvantages.

Once you have carried out your primary research you will need to collate your findings (your data). Guidance for collating data can be found in Chapter 7.

INTERVIEWS

When and how to use interviews

Interviews are useful for both quantitative and qualitative research, depending on the questions asked. Interviews can be either structured or unstructured (see Figure 2.1), and can also be a mixture of both. Interviews are particularly useful if you are trying to find out people's individual opinions or experiences (a qualitative approach). Interviews will usually be set up in advance, but occasionally you may carry out an 'on-the-spot' interview, where you ask people at random to participate.

Example

An 'on-the-spot' interview may involve standing outside a supermarket (having gained permission to do so from the manager) and asking shoppers to answer a question or a few short questions, as in the example regarding parental choice for four-year-olds in Chapter 1. You need to plan for this in advance and give the same level of consideration to what you aim to achieve as you would for a one-to-one interview.

Carrying out a survey on the street needs to be thought out carefully

Structuring your interviews

The level of structure to an interview can be drawn as a continuum (a line upon which we can mark differing positions):

•_____•
Structured interviews   Unstructured interviews

Structured interviews

This is a formal approach whereby the interview follows a preset course of questions for everyone being interviewed. It can be particularly useful if you are taking a quantitative (counting) approach. Answers can be controlled by forming questions which do not allow for the topic to be expanded upon. These are known as **closed questions**. Further discussion of closed questions will be found on page 26 in relation to designing a **questionnaire**.

Advantages
- The questions are firmly set in advance.
- All participants are asked the same questions.

Disadvantages
- There is no flexibility.
- The additional information a participant may have available will be missed.

Unstructured interviews

The unstructured interview is a far more relaxed process, open to discussion and further development of the subject. Each participant is asked the same set of questions but there is an allowance for each question to be developed further if appropriate.

Advantages
- The questions set in advance are used simply as a guide or prompt.
- Flexibility is offered to explore points further if appropriate.

Disadvantages
- Not all participants are asked exactly the same questions.
- Questions about the reliability of the outcomes may be raised.
- The interview can become simply a 'chat' if not carefully controlled.

A combined approach

Often, the most successful method, particularly for first-time researchers, is to use a balance of both styles. This would usually mean having a set list of questions which you as the interviewer are willing to expand upon where it is felt appropriate. This would help you to remain in control of the interview whilst introducing some degree of flexibility. This would therefore place the interview nearer the middle of the continuum.

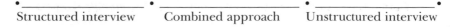

Structured interview   Combined approach   Unstructured interview

Length of interviews

It is advisable to keep interviews as short as possible. Many professional researchers impose time limits, and you should too. You will find it easier to obtain willing participants if they do not have to give up too much of their time. A structured interview will usually take less time than an unstructured interview because of the preset process involved. You should set a guideline for the length of interview in advance, and participants need to know this before agreeing to take part. Even when carrying out unstructured interviews there should be a firm limit on the maximum time it should take (see the example below). One hour should be the absolute maximum. On-the-spot interviews need to be kept very brief. It is worth asking yourself how much time you would be willing to give up for someone else's research. You should not be asking more from others than you would be willing to give yourself.

Example
The following guidelines should help you plan your research and manage your time too.

An 'on-the-spot' interview	2–5 minutes maximum
Structured interviews	15–30 minutes maximum
Unstructured interviews	15–45 minutes (1 hour as absolute maximum)

REMEMBER

A lengthy interview means a lot of time spent by you as the researcher too, in writing up and analysing your findings. You need to take this into account when considering how you will manage your time effectively.

Making a record of the interview
The most common method of recording an interview is to take notes of what is being said throughout. If you are able to use shorthand, this will be an advantage. If not, it can be useful to develop your own version of a shorthand system. This will help you to abbreviate what is being said and therefore write your notes more quickly, whilst still being able to understand what you have written when you come to read it through later on. In a structured interview you are unlikely to have any significant problems as most responses will be short and often limited in scope. An unstructured interview can be more difficult because of the possibly greater variety of questions that develop. It can be helpful to use subheadings within your notes. These break up the notes and help you make sense of material quickly as you scan through them. Be systematic at all times. Use the same approach to each set of interview notes. This will make it easier to compare responses between participants.

REMEMBER

It is important that you allow enough time following an interview to write up your notes. It is very easy to forget the details of what was said to you. Be clear about how your notes will be set out.

Using tape recorders and/or video recorders
An alternative method of recording is to use a tape recorder or video recorder. If you choose to interview using this method you will need to ensure that the interview takes place in a quiet, undisturbed setting. It is important that

participants have agreed to be recorded in advance and have had the option to refuse. Lack of agreement at the last moment will mean you will need to make (unplanned for) written notes throughout the interview. This could affect the flow of the interview process and consequently your outcomes. It is also completely inappropriate to record an interview covertly (without the participants' knowledge). The issue of **confidentiality** should be borne in mind at all times, as should the security of any recorded tapes.

Covert video recording is unethical

Recorded interviews can be useful if it is important to your research that you record answers word for word (verbatim). With a video you may also be able to look at body language or hand gestures used by both yourself and your participants. This is, however, a time-consuming method, needing careful writing up afterwards. It should be selected with caution.

Activity
It can be useful to try transcribing from a tape you already have to see for yourself how long it would take you. Remember that a professional tape will usually offer greater clarity than the home-recorded tape which you would be using during an interview.

The advantages are:
■ You do not need to write during the interview.
■ You can concentrate on listening to the participant.
■ You know you will have accurate responses recorded.

The disadvantages are:

- Participants may feel embarrassed or inhibited by a tape recorder or video recorder.
- Interviews cannot easily be classed as anonymous if recorded.
- Responses may flow less easily because of the inhibitions of your participants.
- Quality of sound is often a problem.
- Problems with recording may mean you have nothing to transcribe.
- Transcribing the tape (writing up the interview) is extremely time-consuming.

Making transcripts

When transcribing the tape (writing out what you have recorded), it is important that you take down what is said word for word. You will need to analyse the responses separately soon afterwards. Interpreting the data as you transcribe it may mean that what you write is not fully accurate and may therefore invalidate the outcomes.

Find a quiet place in order to carry out your interviews

Leading questions and bias

At times our views on a subject can be very strong. This can be difficult to hide whilst carrying out an interview. It is important that we keep our views private to avoid bias within our research. Bias could involve us in leading participants' answers by setting our questions at a particular angle, or by asking questions in a particular manner.

Example

To ask the question

> Do you not agree that fathers should be allowed the same level of paid paternity leave as women have maternity leave?

is leading and also leans toward bias. The participant (or interviewee) may well feel that they are expected to agree. However, paternity rights are clearly not a straightforward issue and there are many practical and economic arguments to be explored.

> The question would have been far better asked in the following manner:

> Do you consider that new fathers should be given paid paternity leave? If yes, how much leave do you consider is appropriate?'

This question does not indicate bias and offers the opportunity for free expression.

Relating to your participants

Many people will be apprehensive about being interviewed. It may be the first time they have been involved in anything to do with a research project. As the interviewer it is your role to make them feel at ease. It is easy to underestimate the level of power you have when carrying out an interview. You are in control for a variety of reasons:

- You have set up the interview.
- You have written the questions.
- You will control the questions.
- You will (probably) have set up the venue.
- You will control the pace and length of the interview.

Carrying out an interview

Many interviews can be quite passive from the participant's point of view. Where possible, negotiate arrangements with your participant to help them feel more involved.

Summary: interviews
There are advantages and disadvantages in using interviews.

Advantages
■ Topics can be explored in considerable depth with each individual participant.
■ The structure and outcomes can be either narrowly or broadly focused.
■ Time management can be carefully controlled by the researcher (but see below).

Disadvantages
■ The lack of **anonymity** may restrict some of the answers given.
■ Time management may be thrown out if interviews need to be rescheduled.

With a structured interview the questions are set and the interviewer would not usually move away from them. This has the benefit of ensuring that all participants are asked exactly the same questions. However, a structured interview lacks flexibility and therefore it could mean that all relevant material is not gathered. Some participants might have been able to offer extra information if a more flexible (or unstructured) approach had been taken.

The unstructured interview is usually based very loosely on a set of questions or prompts for the interviewer to refer to. This is in many ways the opposite of the structured approach described above, in that it offers flexibility. Nevertheless, this approach does not ensure that all participants are asked the same questions. This can raise questions about the reliability of any outcomes of the research and is an important issue for consideration.

One of the main issues relating to interviews is that anonymity is not possible. This may detract from the quality and accuracy of the information given. Issues of accuracy (or validity) are discussed in Chapter 6.

QUESTIONNAIRES

There are many points for consideration when planning a questionnaire. It can often seem the easiest method of gathering primary data, but questionnaires are not as easy to produce as they may look. You will need to consider:
■ why you want to use a questionnaire
■ when to use questionnaires
■ how many questions you will use
■ the positioning of your questions
■ writing open and closed questions
■ piloting your questionnaire
■ how you will get your questionnaires distributed and returned

- categories of response
- using appropriate language
- selecting your target group
- the use of 'on-the-spot' interviews.

Why do you want to use a questionnaire?

A common reason for choosing to carry out a survey is that 'everyone else' is. Clearly this is not sensible. You need to be able to justify to yourself why and how this method would enhance the outcomes of your work. Ask yourself:

- What extra information would it enable you to gather?
- Could you obtain this information from another source? If yes, from where?
- In what way would your project be lacking without it?
- Would including a survey add quality to your work or just quantity?

It is important that you know your reasons and that you are clear that the information you are likely to gain could not be better collected in another way. Keep your questionnaire simple. This is an important point to remember, as the questionnaire will be easier for you to understand and easier for your participant to fill in.

Postal surveys can be expensive

When to use questionnaires

Questionnaires can be an ideal method of gathering primary data if you are seeking the views of many people, or if your subject area could be deemed sensitive. With sensitive subject areas, offering anonymity which can be guaranteed through using a survey can be an important consideration in your decision on how best to obtain the information you need. You may also have a time restriction which leads you to decide that, whereas an interview could be appropriate for your subject area, carrying out the interviews would take up too much of your limited time. Questionnaires can be distributed in a variety of ways. They can be sent by post, handed out personally or handed out by a willing volunteer (for example the supervisor of a nursing home or day nursery).

How many questions?

Questions must all be relevant. If you cannot justify to yourself the value of a particular question, it probably should not be included. Questions should flow into each other. They should follow a logical sequence and not jump from one topic to the next.

The wording of questions must be clear. Keep your questionnaire as short as possible to encourage people to complete it fully. A lengthy questionnaire can be very off-putting. Have a look at the examples in Figures 2.1 to 2.5.

Activity

Consider each of the questionnaires you have just read. Decide the following:

1   How would you feel if asked to complete them?
2   Did they look easy or complex to complete?
3   Did they make sense?
4   Did you identify any ambiguities or irrelevant questions?
5   Was it made clear how you should record your answers?
6   Which would you be most happy to complete?
7   Which would you be least happy to complete?
8   Why have you made each of the above decisions?

Keep these questionnaires in mind as you read through the rest of this section. Think about how you could improve upon them in light of what you have read.

Positioning your questions

When setting out your questions it is wise to ask the most important questions near the beginning if you can. This would normally mean that even if your participant abandoned the questionnaire part way through, you would still have some of the responses you needed most. This is particularly important if your subject area is a sensitive one. At times participants may elect to avoid some questions for a variety of reasons (usually unspecified). Again, this happens more often after they have completed part of the questionnaire.

Survey on Children's TV

Do you have children?
Yes .... No ....

How many? ....

Which age groups?
0–2 3–4 5–7

How many hours of TV do they watch on average per week?
0–5 5–10 10–15 15–20 more

What are your children's favourite programmes?

....

....

Please tick relevant box giving your opinions of children's programmes

Programme	Good	Average	Unsuitable	Don't know
Woof				
Turtles				
Scooby Doo				
Pingu				
Moomins				
Bugs Bunny				
Children's Ward				
Tin Tin				
Dennis				
Tom and Jerry				
Captain Zed				
Mork and Mindy				
Batman				
Laurel and Hardy				
Henry's Cat				
Bodger and Badger				
Adams Family				
Wizadora				
Wowser				
Sooty and Co.				

Do your children watch any that you consider unsuitable?
Yes .... No ....

Do you think that violent TV affects children's behaviour?
Yes .... No .... No opinion ....

If yes in what way?

Thank you for your cooperation

Figure 2.1 Example of a questionnaire (1)

Local Park Survey

We are students from the local college doing a BTEC Nursery Nurse course and we would like to know about your views on the park and its facilities.

1. How many children do you have?

2. What age are your children?

3. How often do you use the park?

4. Are the activities in the park suitable for your children's needs and age?

5. Do you think the park and its facilities are safe for children?

6. Do you think there should be toilet facilities and a telephone next to the park?

7. Do you think there should be a zebra crossing next to the park?

Thank you for your time and for helping us with our questionnaire.

Figure 2.2   Example of a questionnaire (2)

We are
WHH

NHS

**Warrington and
Halton Hospitals**
NHS Foundation Trust

Writing a Research Proposal

What is a research proposal?

A research proposal is a concise summary of your research – try to limit it to 1500 words.

It is an initial set of ideas for a research study which are supported by a **literature review** and /or a **pilot study** or a **feasibility study.**

Proposals should be concise and must address **what** you plan to achieve, **why** you want to research this and **how** you are going to do this.

To begin you should think about your research question – what do you really want to know more about? Your research question should lead to the creation of **new knowledge and understanding**.

What is a research protocol?

- A research protocol is a detailed set of activities for the project you are proposing.
- Activities in your protocol are supported by evidence from previous research but also show how the fill existing gaps in knowledge.
- The protocol is a timetable and guide to your research and shows what you are planning to achieve and how.
- Above all protocols demonstrate evidence of planning, including anticipation of potential problems and how you plan to deal with these.

For more information and advice, contact Research & Development on 01925 662946 or 01925 275514

The Knowledge and Evidence Service can help with literature searching to ensure your proposal is evidence based and that the same research hasn't been done before. Contact the team on 01925 66 2128 or email library@whh.nhs.uk

How do I tell if my research idea is sound?

Does your proposal make a strong argument and show the importance of the research from a health, societal and economic viewpoint?

Have you shown where there are gaps in the existing knowledge and how your research will address these?

Does the proposal frame the issues in a way that makes them amenable to research using the methodologies and design proposed?

Does the research address key questions in the field?

Are your aims and objectives clearly defined?

How will you tell if your research findings are significant?

Are my methods sound and appropriate?

Are the study design and methods fully described, explained and justified? Will the design and methods of the study deliver the aims and objectives?

Have you shown that the design and methods of the proposed research are the most efficient to deliver the aims and objectives?

Does the proposed study design take into account issues of representativeness?

Have you shown how you will address bias?

Does your study meet relevant and legislative requirements?

Has your proposal addressed the benefits of the study?

Is my study practical and feasible?

Have you describe the study in enough detail for an external person to be able to determine the feasibility of it?

Is it possible to complete the study to the timescale given?

Is it possible to complete the study with the resources described in the proposal?

Are recruitment rates realistic?

Are travelling estimates realistic?

Do you or does your study team have all the relevant knowledge and expertise to complete the project?

Title
The title should be comprehensive enough to explain the nature of the research, whilst being concise and to the point.
Many research studies develop an acronym that can be used for easy identification, this is included as part of the study title.

Investigators Details
All investigators should be named and their contact details given, you may wish to include the CVs of each of your investigators as an appendix.

Background and Rationale
Explain the background and context of your proposed research. Here you will include details of the literature review you carried out, and summarise the published literature that supports your research idea. You should show where the gaps are in current research and make a case to show how your proposed research will provide the knowledge to bridge these gaps. You must make a convincing case as to why your research would create valuable and useful knowledge and the potential impact of your study findings.

WHH Knowledge and Evidence Service are happy to help with any literature searches that you may require as part of this process.

Research Questions
Here you need to formulate your research questions clearly. You should have an answerable question that is clear and sufficiently focused for you to do the research described. You may wish to bring in a hypothesis at this stage.

Aims and Objectives
Outline concise and precise objectives that should follow on from the hypothesis.

Study Design and Methodology

Study Design What study design is most appropriate to answer your particular research question?
Setting Where will the research take place? Will your research take place over multiple sites? Will your research take place in a clinical, care or home setting?
Participants/Patients Detailed information regarding your participants should be given. This can include the population from which your participants will be drawn – why did you decide to recruit these people?
How will you identify participants and how will you recruit them?
What are you inclusion and exclusion criteria for the study?
How many people do you need to recruit onto your study – have you used a sample size calculation to ascertain this – if not why not?
You may also wish to describe the criteria for participation or completion of the study, whether you have any participant retention strategies in place. If you have already developed consent forms and participant information leaflets for your study, reference these here and attach these as appendices.
Randomisation Methods Some research studies require a random allocation of patients to the different experimental groups or interventions. You will need to explain what randomisations methods you will use.

Methods of Assessment or Measurement How will you collect data, what instruments will be used to collect data – why are these suitable?

Outcome Measures/Objectives The measurement outcomes used to support or reject the hypotheses can be stated and separated into primary and secondary outcomes.

Interventions (If applicable) A description of the study intervention should be provided. If you are giving a treatment or investigation, the dose, timing, method of providing, administering and receiving the treatment should be detailed. All necessary safeguards and potential risks should be made clear, including the methods by which intervention will be monitored.

Ethical Consideration

You should read any appropriate ethical guidelines and ask yourself how/whether your project follows these. You should familiarise yourself with all of WHHs governance and ethical approvals necessary for conducting research within the Trust when you begin to design your study. Obtaining the correct approvals can be time consuming and this should be taken into account when developing the timescales of the study.

All ethical concerns should be outlined here. You should explain the methods by which participant's interests will be safeguarded. Examples of this include the process of risk limitation, how you will maintain confidentiality or anonymise patient's data and how you will monitor any adverse side effects.

Timescales

It is important to map out a reasonable timeline for your research that takes into account all processes from planning to dissemination. This timeline will serve as a monitoring tool, allowing you (and external monitors) to see whether the research is progressing in line with what was expected.

Start with your intended finishing date and do not underestimate the amount of time that it takes to finalise your drafts into a finished product. Remember here to take into account the fact that things may go wrong, be realistic with time frames for recruitment, make sure you factor in travel time (if necessary). If you are carrying out interviews you will want to factor in transcription time, if you are carrying out questionnaires don't forget that data entry may be required.

It may be useful here to develop a Gantt Chart, this helps you to visually see what your research timeline will look like.

Dissemination

Think about how you can ensure that your findings have maximum research impact.

What are you hoping to do with your research findings? Could this lead to a potential publication and if so where?

If you are planning to publish – think about who can review your work and provide feedback on it. This can be your peers as well as people more experienced than you.

Could you create a poster presentation of your research to present at relevant conferences?

Are you planning to hold a dissemination event, whereby you inform people about the research and what you have found out? Who might be key to include in such an event – would this be an opportunity to involve wider stakeholders/commissioners in the field?

Are you planning to develop any publicity to disseminate your findings?

Questionnaire

Comparison of 4 local playgrounds

Parents

1 How many children do you have?

2 What ages are they?

3 Do you always use this park?

4 Why?

5 Are you satisfied with the cleanliness of the park?

6 Where are the nearest toilets? Are they hygienic?

7 How do you travel here?

8 How many times do you visit here a week?

9 If you use a car, is the parking adequate?

10 Do you feel that the equipment and area are safe?

11 Are dogs allowed?

12 Would you like to see anything added or changed?

Children

1 What do you like to play on the best?

Figure 2.3 Example of a questionnaire (3)

Sex Education Questionnaire

We are students from the local college studying for a diploma in Nursery Nursing and as part of our current classes we have been asked to carry out a questionnaire about people's views on Sex Education for Children.

1. At what age do you feel sex education should be taught?
    Unders 7 ❏ 7–9 ❏ 9–11 ❏ Secondary school age ❏

2. Who do you think should be responsible for teaching sex education?
    Teacher ❏ Parent ❏ Health Visitor ❏ Trained specialist ❏

3. Would you like to see the videos and materials to be used in your child's school in advance of the lessons?

4. Should boys and girls be taught separately?

	Single	Mixed
Under 7	❏	❏
8–9	❏	❏
9–11	❏	❏
Secondary school age	❏	❏

5. If in school should parental consent be given in advance to the lessons?
    YES ❏ NO ❏

6. Are you aware of the age at which your child has had/will have sex education lessons?
    YES ❏ NO ❏

7. If you answered yes to question 6, then at what age?
    . . . . . yrs

8. Do you agree that the emotional content is as important as the biological aspect?
    Strongly agree   ❏
    Agree   ❏
    Disagree   ❏
    Do not know   ❏

Figure 2.4   Example of a questionnaire (4)

Shopping Survey

1. What is your age?   ≤ 20 ❑   20–30 ❑   30–40 ❑
   40–50 ❑   50–60 ❑   60–70 ❑   70+ ❑

2. What is your marital status?

   Married ❑ Single ❑

3. Have you any dependent children? YES / NO
   If yes, how many? 1 2 3 4 5 6 7 or more?

4. How long have you lived in this area?   _____ years

5. Where do you buy your main groceries?

   _____

6. Have you always shopped there?
   YES / NO

7. Do you know, or are you known by, the shop assistants?
   YES / NO

8. Do you consider shopping to be a tedious necessity or do you gain
   enjoyment from it?
   YES / NO / DON'T KNOW

Figure 2.5   Example of a questionnaire (5)

Keep questionnaires as short as possible

Questions must be carefully thought through. They should not offend or pry into an individual participant's privacy. When carrying out a survey as part of a course of study, it is important that you ask your tutor to look at your proposed questionnaire before it is distributed (or photocopied). Your tutor will be able to guide you if any questions are inappropriate.

Open and closed questions

An **open question** offers the opportunity for an individual answer. A **closed question** restricts the participant's answer to one word or statement.

You need to decide which form of question is appropriate for your questionnaire before you start writing it. A combination of both may well be the answer. This would give you control over some aspects of your questionnaire (the closed questions gaining you some 'core' information). More flexibility could then be achieved by using open questions to allow participants to express their views freely.

Consider the examples set out below.

Example

'Do you enjoy the meals here?' is a closed question. 'Yes' or 'No' might easily be the answer offered. Whereas 'Which meals do you prefer here?' offers the opportunity for a range of answers and therefore extends conversation and increases the questioner's understanding of the level of satisfaction regarding mealtimes experienced by the participant.

Activity

1   Decide whether the following questions are open or closed.
   a) Have you had a visitor today?
   b) Do you enjoy listening to the radio?
   c) Which are your favourite television programmes?
   d) Do you enjoy stories?
   e) Are you playing with the train set?
   f) Which park do you enjoy going to most?
2   How could you alter the closed questions to make them into open questions?

Always re-read and check the questions in your survey. Read them aloud to somebody. Wherever possible, ask someone else to read them through for you.
■   Do they make sense?
■   Be sure in your mind whether your questions are open or closed.
■   Will your questions get you the information you are looking for?
Researchers sometimes find that their research outcomes are unanticipated, and perhaps are at a tangent to the main focus of their subject. This can often be due to the phrasing of their questions. They did not get the answers they were expecting because they did not ask the right questions.

Piloting your questionnaire

It is important to pilot your questionnaire before distributing it to your main target group. Piloting means asking a small number of 'similar' participants to complete your questionnaire and comment on the layout, the instructions for completion of the questionnaire, and the clarity of your questions. You will also be able to find out how long your questionnaire takes to answer. Sometimes the meaning of questions can seem obvious to you, the writer, but are far from clear to others reading them. The piloting process helps get rid of any ambiguities.

REMEMBER

You need to allow time for your pilot to be completed, returned and analysed, as well as time to make any alterations to it, plus copying it for your main survey.

Getting your questionnaires distributed and returned

When using questionnaires you need to consider how practical it is likely to be for you to distribute them initially and collect them again once they are completed. Think: will you do this yourself, or is there a willing volunteer who would be able to do it for you? If you are distributing questionnaires to a number of people in a particular setting the latter may well be possible. If your research involves obtaining responses from a lot of individuals you will need to have sufficient time available to you to visit them all, or be able to finance return postage for them.

If you are carrying out all the distribution yourself, you will need to be practical as to how many people you include. It is better to limit the numbers and be able to cope with distribution and collection rather than not be able to complete the process.

Categories of response

You need to decide how your questions will be answered. This is directly related to the issue of open and closed questions.

- Will you have boxes to be ticked or spaces to be written in?
- Should participants circle their choice of answer?

Whatever option you decide on, it must be clear to the participants how they are to fill your questionnaire in. Instructions should be written at the top of your questionnaire.

CASE STUDY

Rosina wanted to find out what level of training day nursery staff in her area had received on child protection. For her 'pilot' survey she asked a group of day nursery staff from a nursery in the next town to complete her questionnaire (Figure 2.6). Her friend who worked there was the 'willing volunteer' who distributed the questionnaires and collected them in for her.

1 Were Rosina's instructions clear?
2 Would Rosina have got the information she required?
3 Were there any ambiguities?

Questionnaire

Thank you for agreeing to complete this questionnaire. My survey is aimed at finding out how many day nursery staff have had training in child protection and whether this is linked to the level of responsibility held.

Most questions require you to tick the appropriate box. If additional answers are required it will be indicated.

Thank you again for giving up your time.   Rosina.

Q1. What qualifications in early years do you hold? Please tick all that apply.

BTEC National Diploma in Childhood Studies _____

NNEB/Cache Diploma _____ City & Guilds 324 _____

PPA/PLA Diploma _____ Early Years Teacher _____ ADCE

BTEC Higher National _____ Other (please specify) _____
Childhood Studies

Q2. What NVQ level is your qualification equivalent to?

NVQ 1 _____ NVQ 2 _____ NVQ 3 _____ NVQ 4 _____ Unsure _____

Q.3 What is your current job title?

Nursery Manager _____ Nursery Supervisor _____ Nursery Officer _____

Nursery Assistant _____ Other (please specify) _____

Q.4 How many staff are you responsible for? Please specify _____ .

Q.5 Who is your line manager? Please specify _____ .

Q.6 Have you had training in child protection?   YES _____
                                                            NO _____
                                                            UNSURE _____

Q.7a If yes, was this within your main training (AS Q.1)?   YES _____
                                                                    NO _____

Q.7b If not, please specify what child protection training you have undertaken.

_____

_____

Please add any further comments you would like to make.

Figure 2.6   Rosina's questionnaire

Rosina would probably get most of the information she required to support the rest of her project. Her instructions were mostly clear, but question 5 (Who is your line manager?) was ambiguous. The job title of the line manager is what Rosina was asking for. This could however have been misunderstood and names of staff given instead, being of no use to Rosina's research.

A scaled response

Rosina could have used a **scaled response** question within her survey if she had wanted to find out to what degree staff felt training in child protection was important.

Examples

Q How important is it for day nursery staff to have had training in child protection?
Vital __ Very important __ Important __ Quite important __ Not important __
Q Training in child protection is very important for all day nursery staff.
Strongly agree __ Agree __ Disagree __ Strongly disagree __
Q Circle the number on the scale below which represents how important you feel it is for day nursery staff to have had training in child protection, number 1 being of lowest and number 10 being of highest importance.
1   2   3   4   5   6   7   8   9   10

Activity

Which style of question (and response) do you prefer, and why? Is one style more easily understood than another. Do you think these questions are open or closed?

REMEMBER

Keep your responses as consistent as possible. You would not usually have more than two styles of response on any one questionnaire.

A ranked response

With a **ranked response** the participant places their answers in rank order.

Example

Q What qualities make a good carer?
Place the following statements in order of importance, 1 to 5.
____ A care qualification
____ Experience
____ Patience
____ A sense of humour
____ A caring nature

Which number did you consider to be indicating greatest importance, 1 or 5? It is important that you always make this clear to the participant.

A category response

At times it is necessary to place answers in categories. Rosina could have extended her questionnaire to include a **category response** question asking how long it was since the day nursery staff gained their qualifications.

Example

Q   How long ago did you qualify?

0–3 years ___ 4–8 years ___ 9–12 years ___ 13–16 years ___
Other (please specify) ___

This would have enabled her to consider links between the responses made and how long it was since the person making a particular response qualified.

Wording questions appropriately for your 'target' group is important

Warrington Hospital Library
Borrower Receipt

Customer name: Sripali Yahathugoda

Title: Research Methods in Health, Social and
ID: B08410
Due: 18/04/2018

Total items: 1
28/03/2018 00:53
Checked out: 2

Thank you for using the
PSP Self Service.

Ensure that your categories do not overlap (0–3, 3–8, 8–12, and so on) as participants will not be sure where to place their responses. It will also make it extremely difficult for you to collate and present your findings (see discussion in Chapter 6). Have another look at the sample questionnaires (Figures 2.1 to 2.5). Had you identified the ambiguities there?

Using appropriate language

Think about your target group. Ensure that the language you use within your questionnaire is appropriate. It can be insulting to participants if your questions assume them to have limited understanding. Likewise, it can be confusing if you make your questions inappropriately academic.

Example

To ask the question

> Do you consider that a child of nine months is developmentally within Piaget's sensori-motor stage?

assumes that the reader has an understanding of psychology. Whereas

> Do you consider that a child of nine months explores through his/her senses?

is a question answerable by most people. The writing of questions must always be closely linked with selecting your target group. This helps participants to feel at ease with your questions and helps ensure that you obtain accurate results.

Selecting your target group

Once you have decided on the subject for your project, you will need to identify appropriate people for any interview or survey you wish to use. There would be limited value in using a group of floristry students to answer questions on mental health issues. Likewise health and social care students would not usually have relevant knowledge of flower arranging and plant science.

Target group checklist
- Do your participants need to have a working knowledge of your chosen subject?
- Do they need to be from a particular
  age range?
  type of employment?
  culture?
  sex?
  area?
  and so on.

■ Questionnaires can take many forms.
■ Be clear what you are trying to achieve.
■ Match your questions to your target group.
■ Always pilot your questionnaires.
■ Make your instructions clear.
■ Avoid ambiguity.
■ Keep it simple. You will have to analyse the outcomes.

'On-the-spot' interviews

If you wish to question shoppers at a supermarket you will need to obtain permission from the management. Select your 'participants' carefully. Consider whether it really is convenient for them before you stop them.

Pick an appropriate time to carry out your survey

Summary: questionnaires

Questionnaires are a useful and frequently used method of primary research. There are both advantages and disadvantages in choosing this method.

Advantages

■ Questionnaires can offer anonymity to participants, avoiding the embarrassment of a one-to-one interview.
■ The same questions are answered by all participants.
■ Your time is used effectively.
■ Participants can complete the questionnaire at their leisure.
■ A good return rate is possible (but see disadvantages below).

Disadvantages
- Return rates for postal surveys are often low (below 35 per cent).
- The cost of postal surveys may be prohibitive for you.
- It can be time-consuming collecting hand-distributed questionnaires.
- If participants miss out questions it can alter the balance of your outcomes.
- Unless carefully set out, questions can be misunderstood.
- Preparation time should not be underestimated. Careful planning is vital.
- Piloting of questionnaires is important.

OBSERVATION

Observation can be an important and useful option for researchers to use as it allows you to see what is really happening. It is, however, not easy and would not normally be favoured by inexperienced researchers. Observation is useful because, whereas when you are carrying out an interview your participant may tell you that they consider X to be their preferred option, during observation you may see that in practice they really follow Y instead. In this respect observation can obtain a truer overall result. Observation is a skill which researchers develop over many years of carrying out studies.

As a first-time researcher it is unlikely that you will choose this method as the main primary source for your project. It is useful, however, to have a look at the observation process and perhaps consider trying it out. We can do this by briefly considering the following two points:
- When to use observation
- Direct and indirect observation

When to use observation
Researchers studying children often choose to use observation as their research method, as interviews and questionnaires are unlikely to be practical with younger age groups. Most early years workers have used observation within their course of study and use it regularly in practice. It is a useful means of closely following the movements or actions of a particular child or group of children. A skilled observer can carry out observations unobtrusively, therefore not interfering with the natural play or learning process. This is an important consideration because any interruption to the norm will invalidate the outcomes of the study.

Researchers using observation either obtain their findings by having joined in with the situation they are observing (**direct (participant) observation**), or by observing from a distance (**indirect (non-participant) observation**). This applies throughout the field of health and social care, as behavioural research can be important within both child care and adult care settings.

Direct and indirect observation
Throughout recent history there have been various studies carried out whereby the researcher lives for a period of time within a particular community in order to find out more about their cultural ways and values. These researchers are often known as anthropologists or ethnographers (people who study human behaviour,

Observation can be direct (participant)

. . . or indirect (non-participant)

origins and social groupings). This form of direct participation is called ethno-graphic study. A famous anthropologist named Malinowski is a good example of this. He joined the Trobrianders community (near New Guinea), lived amongst them and learned both their language and their ways, subsequently writing up his findings into a study. Clearly this is not a research option available to many of us.

ACTION RESEARCH

Related to observation is the type of research used when a researcher wants to study their own working environment. Teachers have at times wanted to find out more specific information about how their classroom functions. This is called **action research**, indicating the intention to change practice following the out-comes of the study. Teachers have used this method, for example by building up a relationship with their pupils and subsequently obtaining their required infor-mation, over a significant length of time. An example of this would be the work of Pollard (1987), whose study of children's friendship groups (Chapter 11, 'Goodies, Jokers and Gangs', pp.165–87) was carried out over a two-year period.

As a first-time researcher (if you do use this method) it is more likely that you will (directly) observe simply by joining a group of children or adults during an activity or part of an activity, or carry out observation in an indirect manner, observing from a distance.

Activity

Consider the following examples. Which do you think would be carried out by direct participation and which by indirect participation? Can you think of situa-tions where participant observation would not be practical?

1   Jennifer is studying the level of recall by differing age groups of children, fol-lowing a visit to the theatre. Jennifer leads the discussion with each age group about what the children have seen.
2   Chris is observing the groupings of children at play in a school playground. He is interested in whether boys play in larger groups than girls.
3   Claudia is watching the arrival and departure of children in a day nursery. She wants to see how effective the nursery's key worker system is.

In each of these cases the need for good observation skills is vital. Without this it will not be possible for successful observational research to take place. Shorthand or a code to enable you to make a note of all that is happening is needed. Observers need to be good watchers and listeners. Their concentration skills need to be good as it important that they are not easily distracted. Many early years workers will have developed the skill of observation during their train-ing. Using this previously acquired skill can be of benefit to them in their research.

Direct participant observation can sometimes be difficult

CASE STUDIES

A **case study** is a study of a situation, for example a group or a family, where the researcher looks at a range of factors relevant to what they are studying. Researchers are unlikely to be able to claim that their outcomes are representative, but they may produce interesting further research for exploration on a wider scale.

CASE STUDY

The Sanjeeri family live near the top of a high-rise block of flats in a large city. The family (mother, grandmother and three children aged one, three and four years) have recently been housed by the local authority following their flight to safety from civil war in their home country. Kazik is a sociologist researching different types of living accommodation offered to non-English-speaking families and the effects these can have on social interaction outside of the immediate family unit.

Kazik interviewed each family member (with the help of an interpreter) and made observations of the children at play.

The above example illustrates how a case study can form part of a research study. It also demonstrates how the outcomes can lead on to further enquiry. In your research project you may want to include a case study to illustrate a particular point. If you are unsure how to set this up, your tutor will be able to help you.

Secondary research methods

Secondary research is the use or presentation of material which has been researched or written by somebody else. As an inexperienced researcher, it is likely that you will use far more secondary research than you will primary research. Your tutor will probably expect you to select one or two methods of primary research (on a small scale) to demonstrate your understanding of what is appropriate for your chosen subject. This will then support your reading of literature and your findings from the work of others.

LITERATURE SEARCHES

One of the main secondary sources of information for any period of study is literature. This takes many forms. Books (both bought and from libraries), magazines, specialist journals and newspapers (daily and weekly, local and national) all come under this heading. Guidance as to the practical ways in which researchers approach and use literature is given in chapter 3.

MEDIA ANALYSIS

The term media is used to cover television, newspapers, journals and magazines. Each offers current information on a vast array of subjects. When you know what your study is going to be about you will be able to access relevant media material. It is important to remember that many media sources portray bias. It is often necessary to explore the alternatives to points raised in articles, interviews, and so on, to obtain a balance of views.

Television

Television documentaries can be a useful source. The range of current affairs programmes will also be worth considering. A useful habit to get into is to look through the week's television programmes in advance. If you have access to video recording facilities you may find it beneficial to record any relevant programmes for your own personal use. You will then be able to refer back to them as you write up your study. The programmes themselves may also refer you to further information or work carried out on the same topic (this information is often given at the end of the programme). Sometimes information sheets are available and can be ordered by telephone or post. Remember to make a note of the programme details. Chapter 4 discusses how to do this properly.

Newspapers, magazines and journals
Headline news usually catches our eye first when we pick up a newspaper or magazine. It is important to look through the index of magazines and journals too, to identify links with your subject area. If your subject is currently very topical it will also be worth looking at the letters page and the 'resident' columnist's comment for the paper or publication.

Specialist magazines for your subject are the obvious place to start looking. You will find it helpful to scan through back copies too (usually stored in libraries). Remember to note down any sources of further information recommended. This may mean writing away for information, or finding a specific book in the library or bookshop. A list of magazines and journals relevant to many health, social care and early years topics can be found in Appendix A.

TECHNOLOGY-BASED RESEARCH

Researchers today have the benefit of using a range of technological resources, for example CD-ROMs and the Internet. The Internet is made up of vast numbers of web sites. It also provides a range of 'search engines' (see below). Additional research facilities include ERIC (Educational Resources Information Centre) and microfiche (a database on film).

CD-ROMs
A range of CD-ROMs are usually held in school and college libraries. These offer the opportunity to explore many avenues of enquiry in a short space of time. Many of the national newspapers produce CD-ROMs of past articles, with updates at regular intervals. There are many subject areas on CD-ROM (for example the human body). These are often interactive, offering opportunities to extend learning by exploration.

The Internet
Research facilities have been extended through the development of the Internet, and the many online libraries and encyclopaedias. From the Internet public library you can access a collection of texts which you can download if you want to. Some are copyright free, but others will be subject to copyright. Always check for copyright status, ensuring that you do not break copyright laws.

It is possible for advanced researchers to carry out surveys via the Internet. Whilst the Internet offers an easily accessible and potentially large target group for research, this approach carries with it issues of reliability. It would not usually be considered suitable for a small-scale study.

As well as being accessible through CD-ROMs, the national newspapers are available online. Their Internet web site addresses can be found printed in each edition of the newspaper. Transcripts from Parliamentary debate (known as Hansard) can also be accessed in this way. This is particularly useful if your subject area is currently being discussed within government politics.

Search engines are programs set up to guide you easily through a mass of information to what is relevant to you. Examples of popular search engines are *Yahoo!* and *Ask Jeeves*. These are often available in school and college libraries.

In many libraries you will need to pay to use the Internet. It may well be worth having a session to familiarise yourself with the process.

Yahoo!

In *Yahoo!* you type in the category you are studying (for example 'mental health'). A large index will appear of relevant topics. From this you select another category. Again a further index will appear. You continue to select and reselect until you have the information you are looking for.

Ask Jeeves

In *Ask Jeeves*, you literally ask the computer a question, to which it will give you a list of possibilities. From this you ask another question, again narrowing down the field of answers. As with *Yahoo!*, this continues until you reach what you were looking for.

Search engines such as *Yahoo!* refine the material with each subsequent search, whereas search engines such as *Ask Jeeves* offer the opportunity to ask further questions, but they are not refined (or categorised) in any way.

ERIC

ERIC can usually be found in the academic libraries of higher education establishments. It is less likely to be available in other libraries. It is a facility which searches for information from the key words it has been given, producing titles of books and details of articles. It does not actually give you the information you are looking for, just suitable sources for further research. For example, if you type in 'mental health' it will give you details of journal articles and publication titles for that subject. You will then need to find copies of each journal or book that you wish to read.

ERIC is only of use to you if you have access to the publications it suggests to you.

Microfiche

Another technological source you may be able to access is microfiche, although not all libraries use this system. It consists of a sheet of film, rather like a negative, containing details of articles, newspapers, books, and so on, forming a miniature database, which can be magnified and displayed by a special viewer. Microfiche is most commonly found in academic libraries in higher education establishments.

Most libraries have technology to help you search for suitable resources

For discussion on how you can use technology to present the data gathered from your research, you will need to refer to Chapter 7. For details of how technology can benefit you in the presentation of your completed study, you will need to refer to chapter 9.

CASE STUDIES

The use of case studies as a source of primary research has already been discussed (see page 36). Case studies can also be used as a form of secondary research, using examples drawn up and presented by others. You can use a case study in two main ways. First, as a point of discussion, analysing the main components of the case and discussing each part, making reference either to your own findings from a survey or interview or to what you have read. Alternatively, you can use more than one case study and identify and discuss comparisons.

STATISTICAL ANALYSIS

Statistics presented by other researchers can be of great importance. You may be able to show how a trend has developed relevant to your topic. For example, if you are researching teenage pregnancy you will be able to see how the figures for pregnancy in different age bands compare, and also the figures drawn up in different countries. It is important to use the most recent statistics you can find. There is little point in discussing the current problem of high teenage pregnancy rates in Britain using statistics from 1995 as your example. Many social statistics can be found in the annual publication *Social Trends*, which also has regional information. Most academic libraries will stock this as it is a vital source of information for many areas of study.

For guidance as to how to interpret statistics, you will need to refer to Chapter 7.

Chapter summary

■ Research involves both primary and secondary sources of information.
■ You will usually be expected to incorporate both research methods.
■ The length and breadth of interviews can be controlled through questions and structure.
■ Questionnaires need to be clear, and piloted and targeted appropriately.
■ Leading questions should not be used.
■ Observation, both direct and indirect, must be as objective as possible.
■ The long-term impact of action research needs careful consideration.
■ Secondary sources used to support research should be carefully selected.
■ Issues of bias must be considered in all that you read and also all that you write.

KEY TERMS

You should now understand the following words and phrases. If you do not, go back through the chapter and review them.

Interview	Category response
Questionnaire	Observation
Closed question	Direct (participant) observation
Open question	Indirect (non-participant) observation
Target group	Action research
Scaled response	Case study
Ranked response	Statistics

The following terms are dealt with more fully in Chapter 5:

Confidentiality	Anonymity

---

3 READING AROUND YOUR CHOSEN SUBJECT

> **This chapter covers:**
> - Why read?
> - Finding the right material
> - Sources of information
> - Keeping records

No course of study is complete without the use of books and other sources of information. Good libraries offer access to computers and Internet facilities, including email, as well as written materials. Libraries have their contents divided up into logical categories. The most commonly used system for this is the **Dewey decimal system**, which divides subjects both by type and by number.

Why read?

All researchers need to read around their subject. You will find that it will help you to understand your subject better, giving you additional ideas from the writing and research carried out by others. It also helps with planning, helping you decide how much time will be needed for each part of your project. This process is known as forming a **literature base**.

> **Activity**
> How else do you think reading other material will help your research? Make a note of your reasons and, if possible, discuss in small groups

Reading relevant literature will enable you to check that the overall aim for your research is realistic. Sometimes you may find your thoughts challenged by what you read. This is an excellent opportunity for personal development, as you weigh up different aspects of the topic in question, both in your mind and eventually in your writing. Discussing different 'sides' to an argument will help demonstrate your understanding of the topic being studied.

As discussed in Chapter 1, research should be as objective as possible. If you try to produce a project purely from your own knowledge and experience, without supporting it with references to literature, your research is likely to become too personal, anecdotal or subjective. It is also likely to mean that your work lacks both depth and relevance to anyone but yourself. It may reduce the level of evidence relating to your personal understanding of the subject area, bringing into question whether your understanding has been extended during your research, and thus defeating the object of the research process. Exploration of libraries will normally be the first main task in a research project. It will support much of the rest of what you do.

You will usually read mostly at the beginning of your project, only searching through the library or bookshop further if the process of your work suggests it is relevant, perhaps as you explore an additional angle to your subject. For example, if you find that your subject has suddenly become a topical story of local or national news you will usually be expected to read, review and discuss media articles within your writing, giving your personal opinions as well. This will make your work very relevant to what is happening at that particular time.

Finding the right material

WORKING SYSTEMATICALLY

The **bibliography** at the back of each book will indicate other publications on the same or a similar subject, and referring to these books can help guide you systematically from one relevant piece of writing to another. You should be able to access at least some of these and, as before, the bibliography found in each can lead to yet more publications. This process is extremely useful, saving you time at the initial research stage, and helping give order to your work. Your project will therefore develop in a logical manner and it will remain focused. A systematic approach to each stage of your project is important, and you will waste time if you jump around from topic to topic.

The Dewey decimal system
Knowledge of the Dewey decimal system is useful to research students in that the system offers guidance within its subject classifications. It follows a numerical pattern. The main classification numbers, together with their corresponding subject categories, are usually indicated above the bookshelves or at each end of the row, with a further breakdown shown wherever needed. The Dewey decimal system is broadly divided by three-digit numbers. Each three-digit number is then classified further by the addition of numbers (e.g. 155.3 or 155.31). For research linked to health, education and care the main classification to explore will be Social Sciences. The overall classification for this is 300.

Using the Dewey decimal system to find appropriate material is easy

Example

If the main number (for a subject) is 362, the publications on related topics will start with 362 and will then be further divided, according to subject areas, as follows:

362.1

362.2

and so on.

This allows a great number of related subjects to be classified together (by the overall number: 362), but also allows a separation of detail (by adding the .1, .2, and so on). You may therefore find that if you need to refer to six books with a range of similar classifications, your Dewey decimal classifications may include, for example:

362.1   362.2   362.22   362.5   362.7   362.71

The Dewey decimal classification number is usually found on the spine of each publication in a library. It is helpful to familiarise yourself with this system prior to embarking on your research project.

In the library of your choice, you will need to find out basic practical information. For example:

- days and times of opening (public libraries are not always open every day)
- how many items you can borrow at any one time
- the length of the usual loan period
- whether you can renew your loan if you need to.

You will also need to find out information about the Dewey decimal system if it is not already familiar to you. You may have only referred to a limited range of publications to date within your studies. Your research may necessitate further exploration of what the library offers.

Activity

Try finding your way around the Dewey decimal system with this activity:

1 What is the main classification for education?
2 What is the main classification for political science?
3 What subject areas come under the (overall) classification 700?
4 What is the main classification for psychology?
5 What subject areas come under the (overall) classification 200?

WHERE TO FIND INFORMATION

The first point to consider, when you are ready to search for material, is where you will gain the most relevant information for your chosen subject area. Ask yourself the following question: What (general) area does my chosen subject come under? Is it:

■ health?
■ community care?
■ childcare?
■ education?
■ policy?

The more precisely you define your project to start with, the more successful your search of the literature (and use of the Dewey decimal system) will be. A successful and focused search enables you to use your time more effectively. If you are unsure what general area your subject comes under, ask your tutor or the librarian at your college or school for help and guidance.

In the field of health and social care and early years, there is an extensive range of publications from which to extract useful information, together with a range of sources from which to gather them:

■ libraries
  public
  academic (college and university)
  school
■ resource centres
■ organisations
■ support groups
■ GP surgeries, dentists and pharmacies
■ health promotion offices
■ the Internet
■ government offices
■ bookshops.

Libraries

Libraries are found in schools, colleges and universities. There are also public libraries in most towns and cities. You need to clarify which you can gain access to. If you are studying at school, your tutor may be able to arrange for you to visit a local college library. Some university libraries allow the public to visit, but often within restricted times.

If you know of a book you specifically want to locate, try to note its ISBN. This stands for International Standard Book Number. This number makes it easier for the librarian to help you. It also helps identify a book if you wish to order it from a bookshop. Different editions of books will have different ISBNs. Many libraries have a search screen set up to help guide you to the material you are looking for.

The ISBN is usually found on the back of a publication

Public libraries
Within public libraries you will find books for both education and the social sciences. They are unlikely to update stocks as quickly as in academic libraries, so if you are looking for a new publication, an academic library would be more useful to you. A range of reference books will usually be held, together with copies of some of the main government papers.

Libraries keep current and back copies of an extensive range of newspapers, magazines and journals. These are for use only within the library reading areas. You cannot usually borrow them.

Academic libraries
College (further education) and university (higher education) libraries tend to keep more up-to-date stock of materials and are usually a better source of academic material than public libraries. Each faculty, school or unit will stock a range of publications linked to the relevant courses and fields of study its faculty offers. In most libraries you will find material covering aspects of early years care and education.

School libraries
School libraries will often have a more limited range of material available, but may be able to arrange access to local further and higher education establishments. However, many government policies and legal positions can be found on the Internet, and this is now available within most schools.

Most libraries have technology to help you search for suitable resources

Resource centres

A resource centre specialising in your chosen topic area might be available. Organisations such as the NSPCC have one. Local authorities with a strong traveller population or other minority ethnic group may have a specifically set-up centre to offer advice and guidance on additional cultural lifestyles. You may be able to visit these centres, or you may be able to obtain information by post.

Organisations

Organisations and charities can be found raising awareness and funding for a multitude of illnesses, conditions and circumstances. They are often staffed by volunteers and have limited spare resources. Whenever possible you should include a donation to the organisation's funds in return for asking for advice and information. Many have web sites which can be found on the Internet, and often you will be able to find what you are looking for without having to contact the organisation directly.

Support groups

As stated above, organisations such as these are usually linked to charities. Support groups are also run mostly by volunteers, and contributing to their funds is important.

GP surgeries, dentists and pharmacists

Your local primary healthcare practice is usually a good source of up-to-date health information. A range of leaflets and booklets on all aspects of family health can usually be found on display, or are available on request. Alternatively, you could speak to the resident health visitor for more specific information. You may need to make an appointment, and clearly their priority would be to their practice clients. Therefore it is important that you make your request in plenty of time. Dentists and pharmacists will also have information on general health care issues which may be relevant to you. Most dental and health care practices and also pharmacies will welcome your interest in developing your understanding of health issues.

Health promotion offices

If you are fortunate enough to have a health promotion office locally you will almost certainly find it to be of great benefit to you if your research is health related. They are often found within general hospitals or in community health centres. The resources they offer are usually free of charge, and cover an extensive range of subjects. They will often provide display material through a loan scheme, including videos, posters and photographic displays.

Many health promotion offices allow you to visit to browse through the available materials, while others have lists for you to order copies of whatever you need. Sometimes you will need to collect the materials; other offices will deliver your selected materials to your local surgery or health centre.

THE INTERNET

See Chapter 2, p. 38 for discussion on using the Internet.

Government offices

Your local MP will have an office in your area You can also contact ministers at the national offices for each of the political parties (based in the House of Commons). Many government documents (white and green papers) can, however, be obtained directly via the Internet, together with copies of Hansard (transcriptions of parliamentary debate). Brief summaries of some parliamentary debates are available on request from party offices.

If your research topic is linked to legislation, this may be of particular interest to you.

Bookshops

Clearly a bookshop is an obvious place to find material on a vast range of subjects. As with libraries, bookshops will order copies of any publication for you. Once again the ISBN will be helpful to this process. If you do not have it, then give the bookshop staff as many details as you can about the publication you are trying to locate.

SETTING PARAMETERS FOR YOUR LITERATURE SEARCH

The extent of your literature search will be largely determined by the scope of your topic area and the parameters you set yourself. Setting **parameters** means deciding how broad or narrow your study will be. Try asking yourself the following questions.

1   What year will I research back to ? 1990? 1980? 1950?
    What will you base your decision upon? Much will of course depend on the
    nature of your chosen topic. You will need to consider what the likely impact
    will be on your overall findings if (a) you restrict your research, or (b) you try
    to encompass the full historical angle.
2   Will I restrict myself to British works? What about European? Should I include
    thinking from the USA? Where has the most (and also the most significant)
    research been carried out?

The decisions you make will have a considerable influence on the outcome of your
work, and you need to be clear about the impact of any decisions you make on this
basis.

Once again, your tutor will be able to guide you and help you make an
informed decision.

PHOTOCOPYING

You may be able to photocopy material, even if you are unable to borrow it from
the library (some books are kept for reference only). You will need to abide by the
copyright laws.

Copyright laws

Details of the copyright law for the United Kingdom (UK) are set out in the
Copyright, Designs and Patents Act 1988. Many schools and colleges obtain permission under copyright law for the copying of some material, for example the
recording of television programmes to show to students, or taking copies of limited amounts of printed material. Libraries normally have an outline copy of the
copyright law on display. It is often situated by the photocopier, as a reminder to
those using it. It is important that you do not breach the guidelines. Ask the librarian or your tutor for clarification of what you can and cannot copy.

Remember! There are copyright laws!

Sources of information

How widely you need to read will depend on the level and purpose of your research, and on which course your research is part of.

SETTING PARAMETERS

Consider the following case studies and decide the parameters (the scope) for each proposed research project.

CASE STUDY A

Sangita has elected to investigate the viewpoints of early years professionals and whether they consider that four-year-olds are better off in nurseries or in a school reception class. There is an enormous amount of material available, which Sangita has already noted from her initial search of the college library, and almost everyone of note in early years seems to have given an opinion on the topic. She is aware that the debate has been raging for many years and is likely to continue. There are articles appearing in educational journals and magazines almost weekly.

1 How should Sangita decide on the limitations of her literature base?
2 How far back chronologically should she research?
3 Do you consider Sangita's project to be broad or narrow in scope?
4 Would Sangita's proposed study be manageable for a small-scale project? If not, why not?

CASE STUDY B

Sharon has selected Alzheimer's Disease for her research project. She currently works in a nursing home for the elderly. She has been working there for nine months. Staff have often commented on the greater numbers of residents who have Alzheimer's than was the case in the past. Sharon thinks it will be useful to find out if there are any medical or scientific reasons for this.

1 What parameters should Sharon set herself?
2 What factors will influence her decision?
3 Where should she go initially for appropriate information?
4 Would Sharon's proposed study be manageable for a small-scale project? If not, why not?

CASE STUDY C

Marcia is considering the impact of increased day-care provision on parent/child relationships. She is struggling to decide how far back she should research.

1   How would you advise Marcia?
2   What are the important factors to be considered in setting parameters for this study?
3   Would Marcia's proposed study be manageable for a small-scale project? If not, why not?

If at this point you have made a decision regarding your subject area, try the following activity. If not, return to the activity when you are ready.

Activity

Having looked at the above case studies, consider the issues raised there in relation to your chosen subject area.

1   How will you decide on the limitations of your literature base?
2   What parameters will you set yourself?
3   Will your project be broad or narrow in scope?
4   How far back chronologically will you research?
5   Will you restrict yourself to British works?
6   Would a European angle be useful?
7   Should you include thinking from the USA or any other country?
8   Is your proposed study manageable for a small-scale project?
9   What has influenced your choice of subject area?
10 Where will you go initially for appropriate information?

REMEMBER

You need to consider carefully the impact that your decisions will have on your overall project outcomes.

DECIDING HOW MUCH TO READ

To the question 'How much should I read?' there is no clear-cut answer. Tutors will be able to advise you on what is relevant to your chosen topic and the parameters you have set yourself. It is important that you take up the tutorial opportunities available to you in order to maximise the support offered. The importance of tutorial support is discussed further in Chapter 8.

Most importantly you need to demonstrate that you understand the topic being studied, and your literature sources must reflect this clearly. Using a large number of pointless quotes and references will not enhance your work; in fact it will detract from it. Similarly, failing to refer to the work of an important theorist would also detract from the value of your studies.

Libraries and bookshops are an enormous source of information

Reading around the subject

It is important to recognise that whilst tutors and teachers expect you to read around your chosen topic, they do not want you to spend a disproportionate amount of time reading, leaving insufficient time for the actual (primary) research element of your work, and writing up. This again is where your initial planning becomes so important. (Refer to Chapter 8 for discussion and guidance on the writing of a timed action plan.)

Keeping focused

It is easy to go astray when carrying out research. Having become enthusiastic about a particular topic it is important to remain focused. Most students referring to this book will be carrying out small-scale research and there will be neither the time nor the word length to go off 'at a tangent'. If this does occur, you will probably find that you have collated too broad a range of material, and may need to discard whole topic areas, wasting valuable time previously spent at the research and literature base stage. Regularly referring back to the overall aim of your study should ensure that you remain 'on task'.

The alternative to reading too widely is to keep the scope of sources used too narrow. This can sometimes occur if the topic studied can be linked to theorists both past and modern-day. 'New' researchers sometimes rely on the original theories, and discuss them in the light of their own findings, omitting to consider the work of modern-day theorists found in current literature. Conversely, purely concentrating on modern opinion can often lack the breadth and depth that would be achieved by referring to the work of past theorists too. You need to get the balance right. This comes with practice, and once again this is where the advice and guidance of tutors should be sought.

As you identify ideal sources of information you need to ensure that you have clearly noted all the details that you require. This will enable you to access relevant material again quickly at a later date.

A LITERATURE BASE

A literature base is simply a systematic collection of material or excerpts from material, linked to your chosen topic. Sources would normally include some or all of the following:

■ books
■ journals
■ magazines
■ newspaper articles
■ Internet material
■ CD-ROM material
■ information sheets and pamphlets
■ government documents and Hansard (transcripts of Parliamentary debate).

This is not an exhaustive list. For each subject area there will be relevant additional sources. It is important to explore as many of these as time allows. There are greater opportunities now than ever before for researching using technology, particularly the Internet (see Chapter 2).

The following activity can form an important part of your initial planning, when you come to start your project, thinking through the different angles you might take and deciding where you can best obtain the material you need.

Activity
What other sources can you add to the above list? Make a note of your ideas and where you can gain access to the sources.

Refer to the list of information sources in Appendix B for further ideas.

Books on health, social care and early years are readily available. Early years has a much higher profile now than ever before, and a wealth of material is available covering all the main issues.

Many early years professionals write in the media, sharing their expertise. They demonstrate how new theories and ideas are linked into, and are of benefit to, current practice, and show how it is developing. These sources of professional insight, as whole books, articles within books, journals and magazines, are vital to students such as yourself carrying out research, whether small-scale or much larger. The knowledge and experience of these professionals reflect what is happening at a given point in time across the early years or health and social care field, ensuring up-to-date findings for your work. New journals are appearing regularly, again reflecting developments in early years and social care. Most libraries regularly update their publication stocks. It could be useful to ask your tutor or librarian for a regularly updated list of what is available.

Many examples from books and journals are referred to in this book, and an up-to-date list of useful journals and magazines can be found in Appendix A.

Keeping records

It is advisable to keep a pen and notepad to hand when researching in the library or bookshop for ideas and sources of information. It is impossible to remember all the details you will need, and making a note of sources saves the frustration of having to find the 'ideal' source all over again, as already discussed.

When making notes from literature it works well if you write using a variety of headings. This breaks up the text and enables easier identification of the proposed link to each particular aspect of your research topic. Consider the following example.

Example
Alana is studying equality of opportunity and has used, as a reference, Hyacinth Malik's book *A Practical Guide to Equal Opportunities* (Stanley Thornes, 1998). She has made notes using subheadings (together with general **referencing** notes) as follows:

What are equal opportunities? page 1

Socialisation: page 4

Theories of prejudice: page 14

Equal rights legislation: page 24

This will enable Alana to refer back quickly to whichever aspect she decides to work with.

An alternative option for Alana would be to have used a small notebook, writing down points about each aspect of her research.

If you were Alana:

1   How would you record the information?
2   Why do you think this is the clearest way?

A useful activity linked to making notes on your chosen subject area can be found in Chapter 8.

USEFUL AND NON-USEFUL MATERIAL

Keeping clear records of what sources of information you are using helps to manage your time well. It is important to make a note of 'non-useful' material as well as 'useful' material to ensure you do not waste time re-reading material unnecessarily. Many researchers use a card index system in order to keep track of their information sources. This is a small box in which a blank or lined postcard is allocated to each source, enabling the researcher to write about a publication and its relevance to their studies, in detail if necessary. Alternatively you might prefer to record details using a computer database.

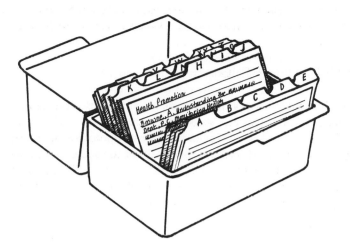

Keeping clear records of information sources and referenced material is important

For a small scale piece of work, however, it may be easier simply to write the out line details onto a chart or page in your file, as follows:

- author
- title of the book or article, including the edition
- type of publication (book, journal, magazine, newspaper)
- date of publication and page number
- place of publication
- relevance to the topic being studied (which aspect of your study might it relate to?).

This is a simple but vital habit for all researchers to get into.

REFERENCING

Referencing means making an accurate and formal note of each source, as above. Referencing correctly is an important skill. The method for presenting referenced material is set out in Chapter 4, which also includes a discussion of **plagiarism** (the use of material written by others without clearly acknowledging it).

CASE STUDY

Sonia has chosen to study equality of opportunity for people with physical difficulties. She has contacted manufacturers that produce custom-made articles for disabled people. Sonia has visited several local stores to assess the potential problems regarding accessibility, and she has also written to local and national support organisations asking for statistics about facilities for disabled people. She has received five replies giving her information which she considers will be useful. Sonia is particularly interested in policy changes in recent years and the impact these have had on public facilities.

Sonia's initial literature search of her college library has led her to Hyacinth Malik's book *A Practical Guide to Equal Opportunities*. This is a Stanley Thornes title, first published in 1998. Stanley Thornes are based in Cheltenham. Pages 43–4 of the book give an outline discussion of the Disability Discrimination Acts of 1995 and 1997.

1 How should Sonia write out the details of this source of information?
2 If you have access to the book in your library, consider how else Sonia might use Hyacinth Malik's discussion.
3 Where else would you look for relevant information if it were your study?
4 How would you set out the details of the sources of information from the replies received to Sonia's letters?

Compare and discuss your answers within a small group.

Chapter summary

- Allow time to visit libraries.
- Use the Dewey decimal retrieval system.
- Search a range of books on your main topic.
- Note those that will be useful – write down the details.
- Keep a record of sources that have proved not to be useful.
- Check each book's bibliography for further sources.
- Ask tutors and librarians for advice.
- Be consistent.
- Be methodical. Work through a series of planned stages.
- Use your time effectively.

KEY TERMS

You should now understand the following words and phrases. If you do not, go back through the chapter and review them.

Dewey decimal system	Parameters
Literature base	Referencing

The following terms are dealt with more fully in Chapter 4:

Bibliography	Plagiarism

---

4 BIBLIOGRAPHIES AND REFERENCING

This chapter covers:
- **Using bibliographies from other books**
- **Referencing**
- **Developing your own bibliography**
- **Plagiarism**

Within your research project, it is important that you make it absolutely clear where the material used in your work has been obtained. This is achieved by:

1 making clear references within your text (the main body of your writing)
2 setting out a clear **bibliography** at the end.

Bibliographies and **referencing** demonstrate the breadth of personal research and reading that you as a researcher have carried out during the process of your study. Referencing the sources you have used to the 'original' work of others gives evidence of your ability to link theories and relevant published material to your own research process.

Using bibliographies from other books

Most books include a bibliography, usually found at the end. This sets out a range of publications relevant to the main subjects covered by the book itself. Bibliographies from other publications provide an excellent short cut to a range of published sources of material which may be relevant to your project. This can be useful, pointing you in the right direction for further material and cutting down on the time spent on general library research. Any sources subsequently used will need to be referenced fully and accurately, in order that others can trace any reused material to its original source.

In order to assess the usefulness of a bibliography, ask yourself the following questions.

1 How recent is the publication?
2 How recent are the books and articles that are referred to in the bibliography?
3 Is the publication directly relevant to you, or only vaguely relevant?
4 Are there any authors cited who have written more than one text on the subject?

Activity

In small groups consider and discuss why the above questions are important.

Think back to the discussion of setting parameters in Chapter 3. The date of publication can be significant as an indication of its usefulness to you, as previously discussed. Remember that a book which is only vaguely relevant to your main subject area is likely to list publications which are also only vaguely relevant and will therefore be of little real use to you.

When you find a book which is genuinely helpful, it is particularly useful to note any authors in the bibliography who have written several texts on similar subjects. It is likely that these authors are well informed about their subject specialism, and it may therefore be worth finding further examples of their work in the library or bookshop.

Referencing

We reference the sources from which we have obtained information for two specific reasons. First, we acknowledge the original ownership of the material. Second, we demonstrate our ability to make relevant links between our own work and that of others. The most widely used style of referencing is the **Harvard system**; another system, sometimes referred to as the British system, is not usually used in schools or colleges but is required in some higher education establishments. This chapter will focus on the more usually requested Harvard system and then discuss the British system briefly, noting the main differences between the two.

Whatever system you use, the most important point is that it is consistent throughout your work.

THE HARVARD SYSTEM

This is the commonly used system for referencing and writing a bibliography. Your tutor will inform you if using this system is compulsory, and whether any variations on it are acceptable. Details of reference sources need to be set directly within your writing (your text). You will need to include the following:

- author's last name
- year of publication (in brackets)
- page number(s).

Example 1

Here we will use the book by Judith Bell, *Doing Your Research Project*, as our example. This is an informative book for researchers, published by Open University Press. You may like to expand your understanding of research further by referring to it.

Imagine you are writing an essay on referencing (in higher education courses you sometimes have to). You could use the following style:

Example 1 continued

In discussing referencing it is useful to refer to Bell (1999, p. 50), who acknowledges that there are:

> several perfectly acceptable ways of recording sources and other informa-tion, and most educational institutions will have a preferred 'house' style which you will be expected to adopt.

As you can see here, the material used from the work of Judith Bell is indented to set it off from the main text. In a typed essay, the quotation is normally single spaced, while the rest of the text is double spaced to allow room for the tutor's corrections or comments. The author's last name is used. The date of publication and page number for the reference are given in brackets.

If at any time you wish to use a direct quotation, but want to omit material in the middle, it should be indicated by using three dots, known as an ellipsis (…). This is useful, and often very necessary if you want to quote more than one part of the material within a long passage of text. You give the first part of your quotation, indicate a gap in the passage by using … and then give the next part of your quotation.

Example 2

Using the same quotation from Bell:

> In discussing referencing it is useful to refer to Bell (1999, p. 50), who acknowledges that there are:
>
> > several perfectly acceptable ways of recording sources … most educa-tional institutions will have a preferred 'house' style which you will be expected to adopt.

The quotation still has the necessary information, but is slightly less wordy. An alternative way of using only a part of the same quotation from Bell would be to add a short quotation within the flow of the written text. It would then be set out as follows:

> When referencing we need to remember that there are 'several perfectly acceptable ways of recording sources and other information' (Bell 1999, p. 50). College tutors will usually indicate the expectations of their particu-lar setting.

In this case, when the author's name is not mentioned in introducing the quota-tion, it is placed within the brackets before the date. On the whole it is your choice as to which style you use and when. A useful guideline for this would be:

■ Short quotations of just a few words or one sentence are best incorporated within your text.

■ Longer quotations should be separate and indented.

Activity

Read one or both of the following passages and complete the activity as directed. Check your outcomes with your tutor if you are unsure.

Passage A
From *Caring for Older People* (Stoyle 1991, p. 112)

> Private residential homes are usually run by individuals with experience in caring or in the hotel industry, but there is no legal requirement for any qualification or specific experience. These homes must be registered with the local authority and are inspected at least once a year, but standards vary enormously.
>
> Local authorities are now required to establish inspection units, independent from the management of their own services, which are responsible for checking the standards in all residential care establishments.
>
> Older people and their families should shop around when looking for a suitable home. They should visit several to compare facilities and, if possible, ask for a trial stay before committing themselves. Recommendations from other people are useful in making choices. Provision of facilities varies, and what may be standard in one home is an extra in another, e.g. items such as soap or fruit. People should be advised to find out exactly what is provided for the money. Families should also enquire about flexible visiting, and ask about the supervisor's training in care.

Passage B
From *Good Practice in Caring for Young Children with Special Needs* (Dare and O'Donovan 1998, p. 158)

> Relaxation and stimulation in a multisensory, or white room, are particularly beneficial for children with special needs. The room decor is white – floor, walls, hammock and seating. There are no windows. Equipment includes multicoloured lighting, water-filled bubble tubes, fibre optics, aromatherapy tubes, different textured collages (at a child's handrail height), taped music, wall and ceiling pictures and a wind machine. Some rooms have a water bed. All the equipment is specifically designed to offer a range of sensory experiences (sound, highly visible, textured and perfumed clues) to children who find it difficult to explore, discover and understand their environment. The combination of light, sound, touch, smell and movement creates a calm and peaceful learning environment.

Assume that you will be writing an essay on one of the following topics:
a) Choosing a residential home for an elderly person
b) Multisensory rooms for young children with special needs.

Referring to your chosen subject and the relevant passage above, complete the following activities.

1 Take a short quotation and set it out within your own writing.
2 Set out a longer indented quotation as you would within an essay or discussion.

Check the accuracy of your outcomes with your tutor or another student if you are unsure.

Developing your own bibliography

Having made reference to a variety of sources within your writing you now need to acknowledge them. The bibliography at the end of your work needs to show clearly each source of reference you have used. It offers your tutor, or anyone reading your work an 'at a glance' summary of all the sources of information you have used and helps clarify the extent of your personal reading and research. It also enables a reader to go back to the original source of your information.

Bibliographies are always set out alphabetically, using the authors' last names. As with referencing, the main system in use is the Harvard system. This is described below, and the less widely used 'British' system is also briefly described.

THE HARVARD SYSTEM

In this method a publication would be acknowledged within your bibliography in the following way:

- author's last name, and first name or initial(s)
- date of publication (in brackets)
- title of publication (in *italics*, or can be underlined in a type-written text)
- place of publication and publisher's name (in brackets).

Example

Bell, J. (1999) *Doing Your Research Project*, 3rd edition (Buckingham, Open University Press; first published 1987)

A simpler system is often accepted in further education colleges and schools, but not usually in higher education. Some tutors will allow a simplified version to be used; some will not. It is advisable to check in advance. A common variation of the Harvard system is shown below.

Example

Referencing would be as before. The layout of the bibliography entry would be as follows:

Bell, J. (1999)   *Doing Your Research Project*
                    Open University Press, Buckingham

Check with your tutor about the preferred method for your college or school.

FURTHER POINTS TO BE CONSIDERED

There can be some complications in referencing and bibliographies. The most common ones are:

- how to reference publications with two or more authors
- how to reference an author more than once
- what to do if an author has published more than once in one year
- how to reference work which is quoted in another book but not available
- how to reference journals, magazines and articles
- how to reference videos and television programmes
- how to reference the Internet and CD Roms

How to reference publications with two or more authors

If there are two authors involved in the writing of a publication you should give both their names in the bibliography and when you refer to their work in your writing.

Example

Bibliography entry:
Hobart, C. and Frankel, J. (1994) *A Practical Guide to Child Observation* (Cheltenham, Stanley Thornes)
Reference:
Hobart and Frankel (1994)

If there are three or more authors involved in the writing of a publication you should:

- give the first three names in the bibliography entry
- use the term *et al.* (which means 'and others') for any other names
- use the first name only and *et al.* in the reference.

Example

Bibliography entry:
Cullis, T., Dolan, L. and Groves, D.(1999) *Psychology for You* (Cheltenham, Stanley Thornes)
Reference:
Cullis *et al.* (1999)

As you can see, this is much less clumsy than writing Cullis, Dolan and Grove (1999) in the text. Referencing that is too wordy will tend to disrupt the flow of your writing and distract the reader from what you are trying to say.

How to reference an author more than once

If an author has written more than one book and you intend to refer to both, your reference within your text would again be as discussed above. The bibliography entry would read as described in the example below.

Example

If studying the medical condition of cystic fibrosis in children you may have chosen to use the following two books, setting them out chronologically (in date order) in your bibliography as:

Dare, A. and O'Donovan, M. (1996) *A Practical Guide to Child Nutrition* (Cheltenham, Stanley Thornes)

Dare, A. and O'Donovan, M. (1997) *Good Practice in Caring for Young Children with Special Needs* (Cheltenham, Stanley Thornes)

Or, if using the common alternative method:

Dare, A. and O'Donovan, M. (1996) *A Practical Guide to Child Nutrition* Stanley Thornes, Cheltenham

Dare, A. and O'Donovan, M. (1997) *Good Practice in Caring for Young Children with Special Needs* Stanley Thornes, Cheltenham

What to do if an author has published more than once in a year

If two books you wish to refer to have been published by the same author in the same year, your reference and bibliography will need to show this.

Example

If focusing your writing on how children under three years develop confidence, you may elect to use the following books by Lesley Abbott and Helen Moylett, both published in 1997, setting them out in your bibliography as:

Abbott, L. and Moylett, H. (1997a) *Working with the under-3s: Responding to Children's Needs* (Buckingham, Open University Press)

Abbott, L. and Moylett, H. (1997b) *Working with the under-3s: Training and Professional Development* (Buckingham, Open University Press)

Within your main text you will have indicated which book you were referring to by adding the 'a' or 'b' after the year of publication. For example:

Abbott and Moylett (1997a, p. 47), or

Abbott and Moylett (1997b, p. 127)

This will enable the reader of your work to identify which book you are referring to each time a reference is made.

How to reference work which is quoted in another book but not available
On occasions you may wish to use a quotation which is cited in another publication, as in the following example.

Example

A summary of research into three different age groups of children was carried out by Yarrow and Waxler (1975, pp. 78–9). This is referred to in Barnes (1995, p. 144). If you needed to quote from the work of Yarrow and Waxler, but could not obtain access to a copy of it, you could write:

> Yarrow and Waxler (1975, pp. 78–9), quoted in Barnes (1995, p. 144), summarised the findings of their research as …

and you would continue with what you wanted to say.

How to reference journals, magazines and articles
The referencing of material other than books is less straightforward, as each one used is likely to be slightly different. You need to give details within your bibliography of both the article you are referring to and the publication it is found in.

The following examples have been taken from an educational journal and from a professional magazine. Note the difference in the way the publication date is set out, how the publication (year date) is always in brackets and how the article is set within 'inverted commas'. As with books, the title of the publication is always in italics (or underlined in type-written text).

Example 1

An article found in the journal *Psychologist*, supporting a project considering mental health problems in adults with learning disabilities, would be set out in your bibliography in the following way:

> Prosser, H. (1999) 'An invisible morbidity?', *Psychologist* 12 (5), pp. 234–7

In this example the author's name (Prosser) is followed by the year of publication (1999) and the title of the article ('An invisible morbidity?'). The publication title (*Psychologist*) is followed by the volume (12), the number within that volume (5) and then the page numbers (234–7).

Example 2

A discussion of research in the magazine *Community Care*, into how the Children Act 1989 has not had the hoped-for impact on the lives of travellers, would be set out as:

> Cemlyn, S. (1999) 'On the road to understanding', *Community Care*, no. 1285, 12 August, pp. 24–5

Here the issue number (1285) is followed by the date of publication (12 August).

The following checklist will help you in referencing articles:

- the author's last name, followed by their initial
- the year of publication (in brackets)
- the title of the article
- the title of the publication, in italics or underlined
- the volume series and number, the week or month and date of publication
- the page number(s).

How to reference videos and television programmes

Television programmes form an excellent source of information for research in the field of health and social care. You may want to simply make reference to a television programme you have watched, or you may be submitting a video recording with your completed research project to support your writing in some way. In either case, as much detail as possible should be given. As before, the detail needs to be set out within your text as well as in your bibliography.

Example

In 1995 the Open University ran a series of televised programmes linked to its course in Child Development (code number ED209). Within your text you would reference as follows:

producer Paul Manners in his programmes on family problems (OU ED209, 14 May 1995) raises the question of ...

and you would then continue with the point you wish to make.

Setting out the bibliography entry for this programme you would write:

Open University ED209 (1995) *Helping with Family Problems* (BBC2, 14 May)

How to reference the Internet and CD-ROMs

The Internet is an invaluable tool in modern research. The range of available material almost unlimited. You need to be aware of the origin of your information or statistics. Many web sites are largely American and may not be particularly useful to you. Referring back to the parameters you have set yourself will ensure that you understand the relevance of what you are accessing.

Some publishers now offer the opportunity to browse through their range of publications on their own web sites. Stanley Thornes is one of them. Details are given in Chapter 8.

Each web site you have used will also need to be set out fully in your bibliography.

One point to note is that many web sites are actively maintained and updated, and can change quite rapidly. It is essential therefore to include the date of the reference immediately after the address (e.g. http://www.bl.uk, 21 September 2000).

REMEMBER

Check for copyrights on any web sites you use. Check with your tutor or librarian if you are unsure.

THE BRITISH SYSTEM

One alternative to the Harvard system is the British system. This system can be rather clumsy to use. Just the name of the author will appear in your text. For example, if you were making reference to the publication *Social Welfare Alive* by Stephen Moore (2nd edition), published by Stanley Thornes in 1998, you would need to include in your text only 'S. Moore writes … '. You would not need to add the year of publication in brackets as you do when using the Harvard system. The main difference from the Harvard system is that in using the British system you need to add footnotes to each page where you have made a reference, giving further details. If you have referred to more than one publication during a page of text, each will need to be included. This means that you have to set out the same details several times if you refer to any one source several times throughout your work. Adding footnotes can be difficult for researchers with limited IT skills. It can also draw the eye away from the main text, disrupting the flow.

Using footnotes

Example

Brendon Harris has been studying the problems faced by people diagnosed with schizophrenia in being accepted by society. He referred to the book (mentioned above) written by S. Moore and a magazine article by B. Prior, and his footnotes were set out as follows:

1 Moore, S., *Social Welfare Alive*, Stanley Thornes, Cheltenham (1998)

2 Prior, B., 'Swallowed up by the system', *Community Care*, no. 1283 (29 July 1999), pp. 26–7

Plagiarism

Once you have mastered the use of literature and the citing of quotations it can be very easy to begin to rely on them too heavily. What has been written by somebody else often appears to be exactly what we wanted to say ourselves. As a researcher you will need to develop strategies to avoid (subconsciously) copying the work of others (**plagiarism**).

Activity

Consider the following passage (taken from *GNVQ Advanced Health and Social Care*, by Clarke *et al.* (Stanley Thornes, 1995), p. 204):

> You have the right to know as much as possible about the causes of ill-health and social problems, and to know what you as an individual may be able to do to reduce the risks. This basic human right was affirmed by the World Health Organisation in 1978. The provision of information on health care, health and safety, and social issues enables individuals both to influence political decision making on a broad scale and to make personal decisions about their own health and lifestyles. Knowledge is power; it is the basis on which people can make informed choices.

1 List the main points of the passage.
2 How else could you express these points?
3 Make an attempt at rewriting the passage in your own words. What else would you add? What (if any) part(s) would you consider necessary to use as a quotation?
4 How would you reference the passage in your work and in your bibliography using:
   a) the Harvard system?
   b) the British system?

When you aim to quote directly from the work of another, you should give consideration to the following, asking yourself:
1 Is the passage vital to my work?
2 What are the alternatives?
3 What is the main point I am wanting to make?
4 Does the 'quote' really fit in with what I am saying?

Making reference to the work of others not only shows your ability to use material sources within research, it also acknowledges the true ownership of past work. Failure to do this is the ultimate 'sin' within research and can get you into serious trouble. Where possible you should write in your own words, offering your views and opinions. It is important to avoid paraphrasing (rewording) what you have read. It can be better to use a short quotation alongside discussion, rather than reword large amounts of someone else's writing.

Activity

Make a list of reasons why it is not acceptable to use the work of others as if it were your own. Consider:

1   Does this matter?
2   Why does it matter?
3   Whom does it matter to?
4   Who loses out?
5   How would you feel if another student copied your work for their assignment?

Hopefully you will have identified that plagiarising the work of others matters not only to the person whose work you have used, but also to your own integrity and feelings of self-worth. In the context of your research your own views are more important than someone else's views delivered second hand.

CHECKLIST TO AVOID PLAGIARISM

- Write in your own words.
- Avoid paraphrasing.
- Never put a direct quote into your notes without recording where it was found.
- Put all direct quotations in quotation marks.
- Ensure all references are included in your bibliography.
- Read and re-read your work before submitting it.

REMEMBER

Tutors are usually familiar with most sources used by their students, and can identify plagiarism quite easily. Failure to acknowledge a source, whether it be a direct quotation or the paraphrasing of another person's writing, may lead to your work being failed. Disciplinary action is also possible.

Plagiarism is cheating, totally unacceptable and will lose you credibility in the eyes of your tutors and fellow students.

Chapter summary

- Referencing and setting out a clear bibliography are extremely important.
- The most widely used referencing system is the Harvard system.
- The British system is also used in some higher education establishments.

- Some establishments allow a simplified version of the Harvard system.
- Getting it right takes practice. You need to allow time for this.
- Plagiarism is completely unacceptable.
- Failing to acknowledge sources of material may invalidate your research grade.

KEY TERMS

You should now understand the following words and phrases. If you do not, go back through the chapter and review them.

Referencing	British system
Bibliography	Plagiarism
Harvard system	

5 ETHICAL ISSUES

> **This chapter covers:**
> - **What do we mean by ethics?**
> - **Ethical considerations needed in research**
> - **Rights of participants**

In this chapter we will look at what needs to be considered in relation to the participants involved in our research projects. This includes people being interviewed, those who complete our questionnaires, and those that we observe, either directly, or indirectly. We will consider their rights, the importance of **confidentiality**, and issues relating to **anonymity**. Each of these form part of the term *ethics*.

What do we mean by ethics?

The *Collins Concise Dictionary* (1995) defines 'ethic' as
> a moral principle or set of moral values held by an individual or group.

The collective term 'ethics' is defined as
> The philosophical study of the moral value of human conduct and of the rules and principles that ought to govern it ... a code of behaviour considered correct ... the moral fitness of a decision, course of action ...

Our definitions, as individuals, of the term ethics may vary slightly, but mostly we will be in agreement. We use ethics as a guideline in making decisions and assessing the consequences that may arise from any course of action, and the decisions we make are directly linked to the values and morals of individuals and society. Ethics, therefore, are about doing what is right according to the majority, linking our personal values, standards of behaviour and conscience to our actions.

Ethical considerations needed in research

In research, ethics are seen as the rules governing what is considered to be good and bad practice in the field of research. To behave unethically during the research process is to behave badly when dealing with the views and contributions of others.

Research ethics involves responsibility. As a researcher you have a responsibility to anyone taking part in your study (the participants) not to invade their privacy unnecessarily or without their specific direction and permission. This is particularly important if your research is likely to involve sensitive aspects of participants' lives. You need to keep in mind that what may be acceptable to one person could be of a sensitive and difficult nature for another. Sensitive subject areas will almost certainly be more difficult for participants to talk about, or answer questions on, if they have personal experience of the situation. Also, the manner in which you conduct your research process will be deemed unethical if you show a lack of thought about the feelings of those taking part and the consequences for them. Your participants are doing you a favour. You must respect them for this and treat them accordingly. You should promote equality at all times and not discriminate against potential participants for any reason.

Activity
Within a setting familiar to you, give consideration to the ways in which people could be discriminated against. Think about age, sex, culture, level of responsibility, and so on. Consider:
1   How could this be intensified through research?
2   How could a researcher minimise the situation?
Discuss your ideas within a group of students.

Keeping issues of equality of opportunity in mind, refer now to your course of study and consider the added issue of sensitivity. You will need to be aware that different people are sensitive to different things. This can often be linked to the past and how well they have coped (or are currently coping) with difficult experiences.

Some subjects are always considered to be sensitive. These include subjects on which people have strong moral and often religious views, for example euthanasia and abortion.

Activity
Think of a range of subject areas connected to your studies that could be explored by yourself or your peers.
1   Which of them might be classified as sensitive? Why is this?
2   How might participants be negatively affected by research in these areas?
3   What restrictions do you think you might find as a researcher studying these subjects?
Discuss your outcomes within your group.

THE EFFECTS OF IGNORING THE IMPORTANCE OF ETHICS

As a student carrying out research for the first time it is likely that your work will primarily be of benefit to yourself, rather than to anyone else. It is important therefore that you think carefully about the way in which you deal with your participants. If a subject is not dealt with ethically or sensitively, it could cause considerable distress to participants and affect the way both you (the researcher) and the research project are viewed by others. Any risks that might be taken during the process of a research project need to be balanced against the benefits the outcomes of the research will bring (this is sometimes known as the costs:benefits ratio). When the project is a personal piece of work undertaken as part of a course, you as the researcher need to be absolutely sure that the benefits (primarily to yourself) justify the costs (primarily borne by others).

DECIDING WHAT IS ETHICAL AND WHAT IS NOT

Research experiments are frequently controversial. We each have our personal views on what constitutes good research, and what is not acceptable. Questions about the moral and ethical approaches to some research programmes are frequently voiced by concerned members of the public.

Activity
Consider the following questions:
1   Is it ethical to cause stress and possible lasting psychological damage to animals?
2   Is it ethical to deprive animals of stimulation?
3   Is it ethical to use groups of people unable to give their consent (for example those with learning difficulties or mental illness)?
4   Is it ethical to cause stress to participants?
5   Is it ethical to deceive participants as to the main purpose of your research?
6   Is it ethical to hold drug trials where some participants receive placebos (dummy drugs) and some receive the 'new cure'?

Set out points for and against each question. Why do you think some people would agree that one or more of the above statements is ethical, while others would not agree? Discuss your answers with another student or in small groups. How similar were your responses? What was the basis of your reasoning? Did you identify any circumstances where your views might be changed? Why was this do you think?

GAINING PERMISSION TO CARRY OUT YOUR RESEARCH

It is important that permission is gained appropriately prior to any research being carried out. If participants are young (school age or younger), parental or guardian permission is needed. It cannot be assumed that children will understand what is being asked of them, nor that they fully appreciate the long-term affects that offering personal opinions or details can have. You may feel that your particular piece of research is completely non-threatening and non-intrusive (for example, asking questions about favourite toys or television programmes), but it is still important to abide by the general principle of obtaining permission from the adult with responsibility.

If you are intending to carry out your research in a school or similarly large establishment, the headteacher or management team (often referred to as the 'gatekeepers' because they give you access to where you want to be) need to give their written consent. They are held *in loco parentis* (in the place of a parent) whilst children are in their care. This permission needs to be arranged well in advance, so again your time management and planning is important. The 'gatekeepers' will usually require full details of what you intend to do. An example of a suitable letter to accompany your aims, **objectives**, and so on, can be found in Figure 5.1.

As a student you are likely to need written confirmation from your tutor that you are legitimately carrying out research. A short letter of proof on headed

---

Date   Your Name

                                            Address of home,
                                            College or school
                                            Tel. no. (if appropriate)

Dear _____

I am a student at _____ college / school, currently studying the _____ course. I have been asked to carry out a piece of small-scale research and have chosen to explore the subject of

_____.

As part of my research, I would like to conduct a survey of people working in this field, and am seeking permission to involve members of your staff. Between six and ten participants would be ideal. Responses can be made anonymously and no names will be used when I write up my research.

I have enclosed a copy of my questionnaire, together with the aims and objectives of my study for you to view.

I do hope you will feel able to assist me. I have enclosed a SAE for your reply, or alternatively you can contact me on the above telephone number.

I look forward to hearing from you.

Yours sincerely

A. Student

Figure 5.1   Sample letter to a 'gatekeeper'

notepaper from your school or college will usually suffice. This is particularly important if you are asking for access to written background details linked to the establishment in question. Tables of examination results of a particular school would come into this category, as would statistics about staff qualifications, in-service training, school attendance records, and so on. The headteacher or manager will also want to know the following details:

- your name
- contact number
- school or college contact (plus tutor's name and telephone number)
- dates of planned involvement by the establishment in question, for example:
  letters to parents (if needed)
  interviews (How many? Who will be interviewed?)
  handing out of surveys (if to be used)
  collecting in of surveys (By whom? When?)
- time plan for your research
- Will the outcomes of the research be available for them to read?
- Who else will have access to the outcomes of the research?
- Will they be identified within the research? In what way?
- If promised, how will anonymity be assured?

CONFIDENTIALITY

Individuals
From an individual's perspective, participants are putting their trust in you as a researcher that any information they give you will be used in the manner agreed. It is therefore important that clear guidelines as to how, when and where the outcomes of research are to be published are set out for your participants. These details would normally form part of your planning. In the case of students carrying out research as part of a course, participants have a right to know what will happen to the research afterwards. Who will have access to it? Who will read it initially? Will it be stored in the college or school library? An individual participant will also want to know whether they will be identified within the final piece of work. If it is agreed that they will not, then it is imperative that this is adhered to.

Activity
1   Make a note of the different ways in which an individual could be identified within a written report following research.
2   How easy or difficult is it to guarantee anonymity?
3   Discuss your thoughts with another student. Do any of the methods of identification concern you? Why is this?

Researchers need to clarify for themselves the different ways in which a participant can be identified within their research, other than by name. If, for example, you are making reference to the local authority day nursery in your area and, when quoting the responses of your adult staff participants, you use the term 'he', it will narrow the field of identification down considerably, as national statistics on day nursery employment would show that there are unlikely to be more than one or two male workers in any one nursery. Therefore your participant will be identified quite easily. Similarly, using initials will easily identify participants with more unusual names. Xania Quigley would clearly be far more easily identified than Sarah Harris.

Most participants in research will talk more openly if they are sure of retaining their anonymity. This assurance will also improve the level of reliability and validity of your finished project (see Chapter 6 for further discussion of this).

Organisations
If the participants in your research are representing, or could be seen to possibly represent, a school or organisation, you will need to have full permission from both the participant and the organisation (as above) before any identification of the organisation is made. Failure to obtain this could result in their participation being withdrawn at a later stage, causing you considerable difficulties. This emphasises why it is vital that the overall management have given their agreement. An unfavourable comment about an aspect of a school, made 'public' through research by one of its staff or a student on work experience, could have a far reaching effect. Your personal integrity is important at all times.

Internal research
If you are planning to carry out your research internally (action research) in your own work experience placement or place of employment, you again need to ensure that you neither upset nor offend anyone, remembering at all times that you will have to continue to work with the staff in the future. Any problems that arise from the process or outcome of your research could have a long-term effect on your relationship with colleagues, and possibly your employment prospects. It may also prevent others from being given permission to carry out their research topics in the future, a privilege which you have enjoyed.

Rights of participants

Every participant in a research project has rights, however large or small their contribution or involvement might be. We can summarise the rights of participants by outlining what they should expect from you, the researcher, unless otherwise agreed. These include:
■ guaranteed privacy
■ observation of their right to withdraw
■ anonymity
■ confidentiality
■ respect at all times
■ trust that their contribution will be portrayed fairly and accurately.

ISSUES RELATING TO COVERT OBSERVATION

It is unethical to carry out research without the subjects of the research knowing about it (i.e. covert observation). This is particularly important if you are researching internally (as described above). Covert observation breaks the trust of colleagues. It can allow access to information which, whilst freely given in conversation, would not be offered in the context of a piece of research. It is therefore not ethical.

BUILDING UP TRUST

Trust has to be earned. It is not something we can take for granted from others, neither is it automatically given to us by others. It is worth exploring what trust means to you. Try the following activity to clarify your own thoughts and feelings on the subject.

Activity

1   Consider what you expect from others before they have your complete trust. Draw up a list of your expectations.
2   Now consider the following:
    ■   Which of these would apply to your being involved in research?
    ■   Which do you consider to be essential?
    ■   Which do you consider to be desirable?
    Note your reasons. Discuss these with another student.
3   Make a note of any occasions where you feel your trust in someone has left you hurt, confused or disillusioned. Why was this? What led to its happening? How was it resolved?

ENSURING TRUE REPRESENTATION OF PARTICIPANTS' VIEWS

The research methods you choose will have an impact on the way your findings are presented. You need to be sure at the outset of your research that your chosen method is the most appropriate one for what you are trying to achieve, and therefore gives a true representation of participants' contributions. Consider the alternative options you could take. Justify to yourself why you are using the method you have chosen. Give consideration to how your participants' contributions may be presented differently. Would this be better? Or just different?

RESEARCH WITHOUT ETHICAL ISSUES

There are occasions when ethical considerations may not really be necessary. This could be the case if you were carrying out observations in a public place, for example watching students socialise around the college campus or children playing in a park. Why is this different? Note your reasons and discuss them with another student.

A SUMMARY OF THE ETHICAL ISSUES ARISING WITHIN DIFFERENT RESEARCH METHODS

Interviews

In an interview situation there is an issue of power. You must ensure that you do not use your 'control' of the situation negatively. Use of leading questions can be a problem, with your personal bias making your approach subjective rather than objective. Sensitivity is needed, particularly if the subject itself is a sensitive one. You will also need to be aware of how the outcomes of the interviews are used and whether anonymity and confidentiality have been agreed. Always take into consideration how the interview may affect your participants.

Surveys

If using a survey (or questionnaire) approach, you will again need to consider confidentiality, anonymity and the sensitivity of the subject matter. Leading questions can again be a problem.

Experiments

Few first-time researchers will be carrying out any experiments within their research project. It is, however, appropriate to look again briefly at the issues involved. As discussed earlier, our views on experiments are often linked to how the experiment might affect the participants, for example the costs:benefits ratio. Experimental research is probably the most controversial of all the research areas, with the greatest level of ethical concern.

Case studies

Case studies do not raise issues of direct sensitivity, as you are not directly dealing with any individuals. You are, however, dealing with a 'real' situation, and respect for those persons portrayed within the case study is therefore still needed. You would not usually identify those involved. As with the methods above you still need to think about how the outcomes of your work will be used and who will have access to it. Awareness of your personal bias is again important and you should guard against forcing your views into your work.

Observations

Appropriate permission is particularly important if you are observing indirectly, or directly, those unable to give permission for themselves. Confidentiality and anonymity are once again a concern.

What do you consider to be the ethical concerns (if any) arising from the following proposed primary research methods to be carried out by a group of researchers?

■ observing children at play in a park
■ observing parents shopping with young children
■ talking casually to parents at a toddler group about behaviour management and then recording from memory
■ joining a youth club or group, organisation or gang purely to get information
■ helping out in a primary school class to observe the classroom management of teachers
■ visiting the elderly in a residential setting to make a study of how well they are treated.

Indirect (non-participant) observation

Within most research components of health, social care and early years courses you will be asked to examine pieces of research already published, commenting on various aspects, including the ethical issues.

Chapter summary

- Ethics is linked to standards of behaviour, our values and our conscience.
- Keep abreast of any issues that you should be considering.
- Never ignore the ethical issues bound up in the research process.
- Always think about how you would want to be treated by other researchers.
- Show respect at all times to those who agree to work with you.
- Participants in research have rights.

KEY TERMS

You should now understand the following words and phrases. If you do not, go back through the chapter and review them.

Confidentiality   Anonymity

The following terms are dealt with more fully in Chapter 8:

Aim   Objective

6 VALIDITY AND RELIABILITY

> **This chapter covers:**
> - What do we mean by validity and reliability?
> - Triangulation
> - Evaluating the validity and reliability of research

This chapter sets out the issues that you as a researcher need to consider to make certain that the results from your research enquiries are both valid and reliable. Ensuring both of these will give greater strength to the points you are making in your main discussion.

What do we mean by validity and reliability?

VALIDITY

A general definition of **validity** is 'the guarantee that whatever is being referred to is both genuine and well founded'. Something is valid if we know that it is true; that it is accurate; that it measures what it is claiming to measure. If it is valid it is unlikely to be disputed. In research terms validity is described as something which actually gives a true representation of what was being researched. It addresses what it says it addresses. We are therefore able to say without a doubt that the evidence (or data) before us is correct. In asking ourselves, as researchers, whether we have produced data that would be considered valid by others, we need to be as sure as we can be that participants have told us the truth.

Any changes to practice in any field or profession need to be backed up by evidence. This is of particular importance in the field of early years and in health and social care. For research outcomes to be considered 'valid evidence', it must also be possible to generalise the outcomes. An outcome will not be considered to be 'valid evidence' if it is only applicable to one research project, or to one sample group of participants.

Obtaining the truth
Obtaining truthful answers from our participants is of major importance to our research, but how do we know that the answers we are given are in fact the truth? The answer is that we often cannot know this for certain. This is where it becomes difficult to claim validity. As a researcher you need to consider how you might influence a situation.

- Would you get the same results if you carried out the same enquiry again tomorrow?
- What about if you tried again next week?
- And then next month?
- Would you get the same results if you researched in the same place?
- What about if you targeted a similar place?
- How similar would it need to be?

This might involve your considering the size of the town or city, the cultural mix, the age range of the population involved, and so on.

What if another researcher carried out the same enquiry? Would they get the same outcomes as you? It is important that you are clear about this. Validity can therefore be linked to what is considered to be true, reliable and retestable.

RELIABILITY

Reliability is similar to validity but in research terms refers more to the method by which we gather our information. It relies on our having used an appropriate research method. We need to ask ourselves:

- Was our method reliable?
- Was it the best method for the subject being studied?
- What other methods could we have used?
- What would the likely outcomes of using those methods have been?

Again, the crucial question is:

- Would we get the same results if we replicated (carried out again) the enquiry?

Successful **replication** of a method of research, more than once, is the only way to demonstrate reliability.

Mostly, this will not be practical for us to do. We therefore need to be able to justify our methods by careful selection of our participants and careful preparation of our questions and observations.

REPLICATING RESEARCH

In thinking about how and where research can be replicated, it is important to consider the following:

- How relevant is the subject to the participants involved in a piece of research?
- What impact would using alternative (groups of) people have had on the outcomes of research? For example, if you used a different age group on the second occasion?
- Would the time of year, type of social area (town, city, village, and so on), racial or sexual mix have any impact? How important is the participants' environment to the outcomes?
- What other influences might there be that could have an impact on the validity of the research outcomes?

Being able to replicate your research helps evidence its reliability

Representative groups

As stated above, it is important that we target our research appropriately. We can only achieve reliable results if our participants (our targeted groups) are genuinely representative.

Example 1

It would be pointless to ask an 80-year-old retired nurse how they found the use of a database compared to keeping ward records by hand if they have had no experience of using information technology. To obtain a suitable comparison you would need to get the views of nurses who have used both methods.

Example 2

If your research is considering the views of parents of young children, it makes sense to involve parents of appropriately aged children in the research process. Alternatively, if research is focused on how education is perceived to have changed in the past 25 years, a range of age groups can offer opinions, but these would most likely need to be categorised, for example, under-20s, aged 20 to 30, and so on, to see how opinions might have developed, generation upon generation.

Triangulation

Validity can be enhanced by the use of **triangulation**. Broadly speaking this can be defined as supporting your findings in more than one way. You could, for example, have used both questionnaires and interviews to ascertain the views of parents about what they consider their children to be learning at their nursery.

Depending on the style of questions you use, this could be either quantitative research, in which you note how many answered A and how many answered B, or it could be qualitative research, if you are not specifically measuring how many said A and how many said B, but taking a general overview of their opinions. You might then support these primary data outcomes with your own observations of children in a nursery setting.

If these three research methods are mutually supporting, and the outcomes are consistent with each other, then the validity and reliability of the research are enhanced.

Evaluating the validity and reliability of research

As part of your course of study you will most likely be asked to evaluate someone else's research project. As you read research undertaken and presented by others you will find at times that the method used (for example carrying out interviews) would not have been the method you would have chosen to achieve that particular aim. You would perhaps have been more inclined to explore it through an alternative method, perhaps questionnaires. In your evaluation (or critique) of their work you may consider that your preferred research method would have generated truer and more accurate data (it would therefore have been more valid), or you may feel that your method would simply have been a different means of gathering the same data (therefore having no impact on the validity).

This ability to evaluate and identify alternatives is enhanced by objectivity. As you are not directly involved with the subject, you can be objective. This therefore enables you to make an unbiased assessment. Objectivity can be important in identifying when research is valid or invalid and when it is reliable or unreliable.

Activity

Consider the following questions regarding validity and reliability.

1   What would satisfy you that a piece of research had been carried out in a reliable manner? Make a note of each point, and compare them with another student if you can.
2   What does the term 'a valid outcome' mean to you?
3   In what different ways can validity and reliability be monitored? Again, make a note of each and try to compare them with another student.

VALIDITY

The following examples are research proposals being considered by students. Having chosen the subject for their research they are now considering the issue of validity and reliability. How would you advise them?

CASE STUDY 1

Steve is currently working with the elderly, many of whom are bedridden. He has set a hypothesis that 'the increased use of fleeces with immobile patients has lessened the severity of pressure sores'.

1   What research methods might Steve use?
2   What will he need to consider in relation to validity?
3   How can he be sure his research findings will be considered reliable?
4   Do you foresee any particular problems with this research proposal?

CASE STUDY 2

Pradeep wants to look at the implementation of the Government's Early Learning Goals and the impact these have had on young children's learning. He is currently on a work placement in a private nursery and intends to carry out his research within that nursery.

1   What research methods might Pradeep use?
2   What will he need to consider in relation to validity?
3   How can he be sure his research findings will be considered reliable?
4   Do you foresee any particular problems with this research proposal?

It is important that research remains objective

IDENTIFYING VALIDITY AND RELIABILITY

When deciding whether the outcomes of a piece of research are valid and reliable you will need to consider a number of points. These include the suitability of the research methods used, the targeted group of participants, and how accurate the data that have been presented are likely to be.

Activity

Consider the list of ideas set out below. These different proposals give you the opportunity to explore the above issues, helping you to consolidate your understanding.

Which research proposals do you think would be likely to result in reliable and valid outcomes? Which would be less certain? And which would be replicable? What are the reasons for your answers?

a) Parents' evaluation of their own parenting skills.
b) Teachers' views on the appropriateness of admitting four-year-olds into reception classes.
c) Residents' opinions of the level of nursing care in their nursing home.
d) Parents' views on the quality of the day-care option they use for their children.
e) Local authority representatives' views on the success of their care in the community support.
f) The proportion of people with asthma in a particular group (perhaps in one family).

1 What are the main points you have raised?
2 Where did you identify issues of objectivity (or subjectivity)?
3 Would any of the above topics been better researched through different (groups) of people?

Discuss your answers with a group of students.

Chapter summary

- Validity means addressing what is claimed to be addressed.
- Reliability is the ability to replicate the research more than once.
- Researchers must be aware of their own ability to influence participants.
- Careful selection of participants is needed. They must always be representative.
- Mutually supportive research methods enhance the validity and reliability of research.

KEY TERMS

You should now understand the following words and phrases. If you do not, go back through the chapter and review them.

Validity   Replication
Reliability   Triangulation

ANALYSING AND PRESENTING DATA

> **This chapter covers:**
> ■ **Different ways of presenting data**
> ■ **Presenting your own data**

Throughout your research, it is likely that you will produce a considerable amount of information. Much of this will be in a numerical form, and is known as your **raw data**.

There are many ways in which you can present these data. You may elect to use tables or graphs, or even take a pictorial approach. You need to be clear in your mind about the differences between each type of graphic presentation, and also be able to make sense of information from data presented in these forms by other researchers.

Raw data are the information you receive on your questionnaires, in your interview notes, your observation notes, and so on. Your raw data are not usually seen by anyone other than you (and your tutor). There are no set rules as to how you should store it. However, it is essential that it is kept in a logical order that you can understand and explain, if asked. Storing it in an ordered manner will make it easier for you to access and return to it when you come to analyse and present it. It is particularly important that you keep your raw data safe until after your work has been read and graded. You may need them as evidence of your research process. It can be helpful to use a separate file for your data, or to use plastic wallets.

Different ways of presenting data

When we read and analyse the outcomes of other people's research, we are often taken through a series of tables and graphs. This tends to be the easiest way of presenting information in a concise and 'at a glance' form. It is likely that you will use them too.

Below are examples of the different ways of presenting numerical data, as:
■ tables
■ bar charts
■ line graphs
■ pie charts
■ pictographs
■ sociograms
■ Venn diagrams.

Styles of presentation can be interchangeable, and at times your decision as to which to use will be based on personal choice. The activity which follows the examples is designed to help you evaluate each style of presentation. Have a look at all of them before you proceed.

TABLES

Tables are the most basic way of presenting numerical or written information. Figures 7.1 and 7.2 offer an example of each.

Although tables are a good way of presenting a lot of raw data, they can also be used to present subsets (i.e. only part) of your total set of information, and as such they are very versatile.

REMEMBER

- All rows and columns must be clearly labelled.
- The source of your information should always be given below the table.
- For numerical data, all units of measurement must be given.
- If rows or columns are totalled, this must be clearly indicated on the table.
- For large or complex tables shading or colouring may help make information more accessible.
- Every table should have a title.

Table 1 Parental responses to child behaviour

	% Positive response		% Negative response	
Type of behaviour	Boys	Girls	Boys	Girls
Playing with blocks	36	0	0	0
Manipulating objects	46	46	2	26
Transportation toys	61	57	0	2
Rough/tumble toys	91	84	3	2
Aggression	23	18	50	53
Climbing	39	43	12	24
Playing with dolls	39	63	14	4
Dancing	0	50	0	0
Asking for help	72	87	13	6
Dressing-up play	50	71	50	6

Source: Adapted from B. Fagot (1978), 'The influence of sex of child on parental reactions to toddler children', cited in Cullis et al. (1999)

Figure 7.1   Example of a table (1)

Table 2 Comparison of three learning systems

	High Scope	Montessori	Steiner
Specific staff qualification	No	Yes	No
Specific training needed	Yes	Yes	Yes
Specific equipment needed	No	Yes	No
Particular daily routine	Yes	No	Yes
Particular teaching methods	Yes	Yes	Yes
Own terminology	Yes	Yes	Yes
Particular method of grouping children	Yes	No	No
Particular room layout	Yes	No	No

Source: Jameson and Watson (1998, p. 129)

Figure 7.2   Example of table (2)

BAR CHARTS

Bar charts are a popular choice for presenting simple data. They are easy to draw and, if done correctly, easy to understand. They are most appropriate for presenting data or 'quantities' for descriptive categories (e.g. the number of people using different forms of transport to reach their local nursery), or data for discrete quantities (how many children are one, two, three or four years old in a nursery). See Figure 7.3 for an example of a bar chart.

REMEMBER

- The vertical axis should be clearly labelled, and the units of measure clearly identified.
- Each bar should be clearly labelled.
- The bars should all be of equal width.
- The bars may be separated by a small gap, or may butt up against each other.
- The bar chart should have a relevant and informative title.

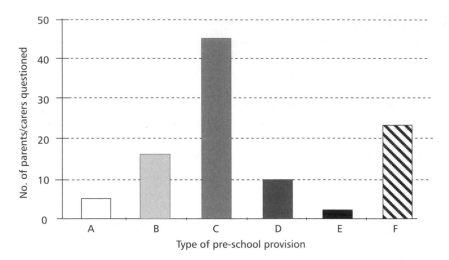

Figure 7.3   Example of a bar chart, providing clear 'at a glance' information of the data collected in the Example in Chapter 1

LINE GRAPHS

Line graphs are a good way of showing trends or changes in quantities, especially over time. They are used where the horizontal axis represents a continuously variable quantity such as age, time or temperature. The line of such a graph is formed by joining a series of discrete points plotted from the raw data collected. Figure 7.4 provides an example of a line graph.

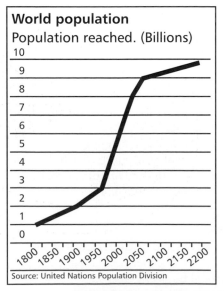

Source: Guardian Education, *12 October 1999, p 9*

Figure 7.4   A simple line graph indicating population development over two centuries

- The horizontal axis needs to be a continuously variable quantity (i.e. it should not be discrete or descriptive categories).
- The vertical and horizontal axes should be clearly labelled.
- The units of measurement should be clearly indicated.
- You cannot plot a line graph unless you have quite a lot of data. Trying to join just a few points plotted from only sketchy data may give an unreliable impression.
- The graph should have a clear and informative title.

PIE CHARTS

A pie chart is a circular chart, and resembles a pie divided into slices of varying size. The 'slices of the pie' represent particular quantities of the various categories that have been measured or surveyed.

There is a specific technique for producing a pie chart, and you should seek advice before trying it. It is well worth the effort of learning the method, and pie charts are a really outstanding way of showing the relative proportions of different categories within a surveyed population.

Figure 7.5 shows an example of a pie chart.

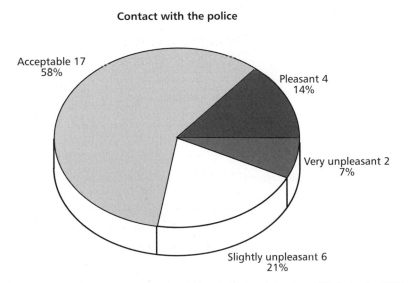

Contact with the police

Acceptable 17 58%
Pleasant 4 14%
Very unpleasant 2 7%
Slightly unpleasant 6 21%

Reproduced with Permission from NCH Action for Children

Figure 7.5   Example of a pie chart, showing types of contact with the police, experienced by 29 children

- The advantage of pie charts is that they are especially useful for showing, at a glance, the relative proportions of different categories.
- Their disadvantage is that they are quite difficult to draw!
- The more categories you are trying to represent, the more difficult it is to draw the chart.
- Pie charts are a good way of showing relative proportions.
- Each slice or segment should be shaded or coloured to distinguish it from the others.
- Each segment should be labelled to indicate which category it represents.
- The pie chart should have a clear and informative label.

PICTOGRAPHS

A pictograph is a way of drawing a chart in symbolic or pictorial style, but serves a similar purpose to a bar chart. Small pictures or symbols are used to represent given quantities, and the resultant chart is divided into rows or columns. If well presented they can be visually striking, and may make more of an impression than a plain chart.

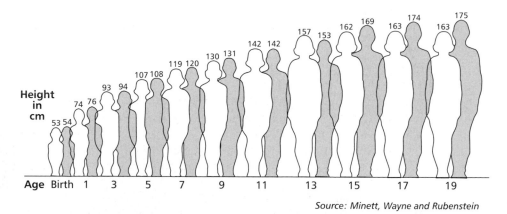

Source: Minett, Wayne and Rubenstein

Figure 7.6   Visual illustration of average heights of boys and girls from birth to 19 years

- The symbols used should be consistent.
- A key should be inserted showing the quantities represented by each picture.
- The symbols used should be connected with the subject.
- Each row or column of symbols should be clearly labelled with what it represents.
- The pictograph should have a clear and informative label.

SOCIOGRAMS

The term 'socio-' means 'denoting social or society' (*Collins Concise Dictionary*, 1995). Sociograms represent data that describe the relationships between different members of a social group. They can be used to depict the social relationships of just one member of the group, or they can be used to show patterns of relationships within the whole group. Figure 7.7 is an example of a sociogram, showing inter-relations of a group of children.

REMEMBER

- The different group members should be clearly identified on the sociogram.
- The axis depicting frequency of contact should be clearly labelled.
- A sociogram is an excellent way of depicting the social structure of a group.
- It can be a useful way of identifying popular children, and also those who may need some help settling into the group.
- It can be misleading, and should be treated with some caution.
- Each sociogram should have a clear and meaningful label.

VENN DIAGRAMS

A Venn diagram shows how different sets of data can be free-standing and can also partially overlap. The common ground (or overlap) is shown by the area of each part of the circles which are linked. Figure 7.8 is an example of a Venn diagram.

Activity
Look at Figures 7.7 and 7.8 on pages 94 and 95 and then:
Consider each example of data presentation carefully. Ask yourself:
1   Is the main information intended to be conveyed obvious to you?
2   What first thoughts do you have about each type of graphic presentation?
3   Is the explanatory sentence accompanying them (where applicable) helpful?
4   Does any one style of presentation appear to you to be more easily understood? Why?
Discuss your answers with another student if you can.
   The activity is specifically designed to help you start to evaluate the presentation of data. It should be useful to you when you prepare to present your own.

Presenting your own data

CHOOSING AN APPROPRIATE FORMAT

It is important that your data are presented appropriately to enable the reader to evaluate them clearly. The style of presentation used will depend on the type of data you have gathered.

Source: Hobart and Frankel (1999, pp 83–4)

Figure 7.7   Example of a sociogram, showing number of times each child in a class was quoted as being the best friend of another child in the class.

The following staff work at Playland Nursery:

Total list of staff	Staff who are full time	Staff who speak Urdu	Staff who are keyworkers
Jamila Marlene Geeta Alan Dorothy Ann Kate Dominda	Jamila Marlene Geeta Alan Dorothy	Geeta Kate Dominda	Ann Geeta Kate Alan Dorothy

These different 'sets' of staff can be represented in a Venn diagram as follows:

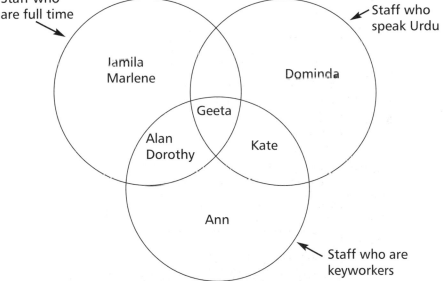

A Venn diagram indicates elements of a link (or common ground) between the features of each circle. This illustration shows that it would be logical for Geeta to be the keyworker for the children for whom Urdu is the first language, since she is the only full time member of staff who is a keyworker and who also speaks Urdu.

Figure 7.8   Example of a Venn diagram

The following case studies are designed for you to practise your ability to present data in various ways, justifying your methods. The case studies involve Donna and Ayshe, who are both studying health and social care. Both students have chosen to carry out research on the subject of disability. Each of them has taken a different aspect of the subject and each has taken a quantitative approach to the primary aspect of their research process. They now need to present their findings in graph form. You have been asked to advise them.

Using the following information, demonstrate which type of graph you would suggest they use. Explain why you would give this advice.

CASE STUDY 1

Donna has carried out a survey, questioning 20 retired people. Each has a mobility problem, for example, severe arthritis, polio and cerebral palsy. Each participant does however live independently. Donna's aim was to ascertain how easy or difficult they each found carrying out their weekly shopping. All shopped in a large supermarket. Of the 20 people surveyed by Donna she found that:

a) Four used their own car to do their shopping.
b) Five were transported by a relative.
c) Three were transported by a neighbour or friend.
d) Six used public bus services.
e) Two walked both to and from the supermarket.

The eight people represented in groups (b), and (c) above needed assistance with their shopping. Two out of each group (a), (b), (c), (d) and (e) needed help in packing their shopping bags. Three people in group (a) needed assistance in taking their shopping to their car.

1 Which form of presentation would you advise Donna to use? Be ready to justify your choice.
2 Set the information out in your chosen form and discuss your outcome with your tutor or another student.
3 Which other graphic forms could you have used?

CASE STUDY 2

Ayshe decided to concentrate on how suitable the facilities in her local shopping centre were for disabled people, particularly those with mobility problems. She visited ten large shops and supermarkets, evaluating the facilities made for disabled people. Ayshe found that:

a) In four shops she had to negotiate a step in order to enter.
b) One shop had three steps up to the entrance.
c) Five shops were either on the level or had a ramp.
d) Eight had a disabled toilet.
e) Three had a low counter combined with a wide aisle suitable for a wheelchair.
f) Two advertised help for those needing it (although all were willing if asked).
g) Three had a low-level cash point outside (again suitable for wheelchair users).
h) All ten had displays or restocking trolleys partially blocking the aisles.

1 Which form of presentation would you advise Ayshe to use? Again discuss this with your tutor or another student and be ready to justify your choice.
2 Set the information out in your chosen form.
3 Which other graphic forms could you have used?

EXPLAINING YOUR DATA

When you add a caption to a diagram, table or graph, it needs to be concise, clear and relevant. All diagrams, tables, charts and graphs need to be carefully labelled with a number and a caption, and then referred to and explained within your main text. Any discussion of the data should be kept within your main text. Refer back to the examples above (Figures 7.1 to 7.8). How clear are they in their present format? Would you have presented them any differently? If yes, what would you have added or altered in order to provide a suitable explanation? Ask another student to consider your ideas. Would they have understood the data better? Would their understanding be just the same? Did they already understand it fully?

BASIC STATISTICAL METHODS

Whenever your research gives rise to numerical data, you will probably want to manipulate or describe the data in some way. **Statistics** is the area which deals specifically with the description and manipulation of numerical data.

For the purposes of your research, you are only likely to need to find:

■ the **mean**, **median** or **mode** (three different kinds of statistical averages)
■ the range (the difference between the smallest and largest result in each collection of data)
■ the standard deviation (how widely the results in a collection of data are distributed, taking the 'mean' as a point of reference).

Mean
The mean is the score which we all usually recognise as being average. We work it out by adding up all the scores we are dealing with and then dividing the total by the number of those scores. For example, in our sample group A there were ten adults, whose ages were:

20, 20, 20, 20, 20, 20, 20, 26, 26, 28

The mean would be calculated as follows:

20 + 20 + 20 + 20 + 20 + 20 + 20 + 26 + 26 + 28 = 220
220 ÷ 10 = 22

The mean age of the ten adults is 22.

Median

The median is the point in the 'row' or 'sequence' of ages that divides the lower half from the higher half. Therefore, again using the ages of the ten adults, setting them out in numerical order we get:

20   20   20   20   20   20   20   26   26   28

The median is the central point:

20   20   20   20   20   20   20   26   26   28

The mean was 22, but the median is 20. As you can see, for some purposes this may be a more accurate description of the age group of these adults.

Mode

The mode is the score (or age) that is the most common in the data. In the case of this same group of adults it will again be 20 as seven are aged 20, two are 26 and only one is aged 28.

20   20   20   20   20   20   20   26   26   28

Using group A in this example the variance between the three averages is not significantly different, but the variance can be more easily seen with our sample group B. In this group there are six adults from one family whose ages are:

20, 30, 30, 30, 96, 100

The mean would be 51, whereas the mode and also the median would be 30. To state that 51 is the average age of this group of adults without showing the spread of their ages would not be helpful, as no one is aged anywhere near the mean average of 51. The figure 30 is also not terribly useful without explanation.

■ Which 'average' do you consider to be the most useful here? Why do you think this?

Hopefully these examples show how misleading statistics can be. Although you do not need to know complicated mathematical formulae (at this level), it is useful to be able to calculate the various averages and understand how they can be used appropriately. It is also useful to be aware of how at times they can show misleading information if read without further investigation.

RANGE AND STANDARD DEVIATION

Sometimes the range of numerical data can be shown on a chart (see Figure 7.9) as **standard deviation**. This gives a curved illustration of all the 'scores' gathered.

Range

The **range** is the difference between the lowest and the highest result taken from your research. You would calculate the range by subtracting the lowest result from the highest.

Standard deviation

The standard deviation is an indication of how widely the results are distributed. If you take the 'mean' as your point of central focus, you will then consider how far to either side the range of results spreads. A small standard deviation would see all the results in a narrow band towards the middle of the grid. A large standard deviation would see the results spread over a broad band on the grid.

Therefore, for the range of results from our sample group A above, there is a small standard deviation, whereas sample group B has a larger standard deviation.

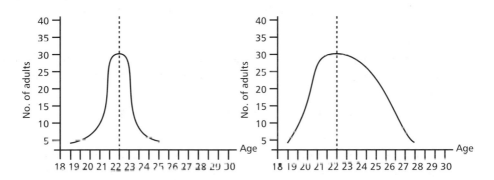

Figure 7.9   Example of standard deviation. A small standard deviation is indicated by a narrow band towards the 'mean'. A large standard deviation is indicated by a broad band spreading out from the mean.

Activity
Using the range of results from our sample groups A and B, produce the graphs corresponding to those shown in Figure 7.9, showing the standard deviations.

MISUSE OF STATISTICS

As has just been demonstrated, at times statistics can be misleading. It is a regular concern that statistics can be manipulated to show one thing, when the raw data really suggest something else. School achievement tables are a good example of this. Have a look at the table in Figure 7.10.

To someone who does not know the schools included in the table it would seem clear that school A is the better school because the results are far better at A-level (80% gain at least three passes at A–C) than those of any of the other schools. This figure is a consistent achievement for the school, and is to be commended.

However, if the table is read by someone who knows that school A has selective entry both at Year 7 entry and again to get into the sixth form (only pupils with five GCSE grades at A–C are admitted), it would seem logical that its results are the best.

Table of school achievement: A-level results showing pupils with three grades A–C

School	1998	1999	2000
School A	80%	82%	80%
School B	61%	63%	63%
School C	35%	38%	42%
School D	58%	63%	62%
School E	49%	51%	48%

Figure 7.10   Table showing that numerical data can sometimes be misleading

None of the other schools has a selective entry at any stage, and school C (with 42% of pupils gaining at least three passes at A–C) has increased its achievement levels consistently over the past three years (35 to 38 to 42%). This clearly indicates an improving academic record.

Activity

Using the schools data above, discuss as a group which of the three following issues is really the most important.

1   The results that the schools achieve at A-levels.
2   The results that the schools achieve at A-levels, given the previous academic achievements of their pupils.
3   The rate at which the various schools are improving.

Information such as this is very relevant to a parent selecting a secondary school for their child, as it gives a truer overall picture.

As you collate your raw data and prepare it for presentation, consider again your personal viewpoints, asking yourself the following questions.

1   Have the results been as you expected?
2   Have you presented the results appropriately?
3   Will the reader of your project understand the true outcome of your research?
4   Has any personal bias been allowed into your presentation?

Chapter summary

● Data can be presented and interpreted in various ways.
● It is important that you present your data in an appropriate form.
● You need to explore any data that you read thoroughly.
● Try to obtain other evidence to back up data.

KEY TERMS

You should now understand the following words and phrases. If you do not, go back through the chapter and review them.

Raw data   Venn diagram
Table   Mean
Bar chart   Median
Line graph   Mode
Pie chart   Range
Pictograph   Standard deviation
Sociogram

8 *PLANNING A SMALL-SCALE STUDY*

> ## This chapter covers:
> - **Choosing your subject area**
> - **Writing your aims and objectives**
> - **Setting out your hypothesis, issue or research question**
> - **Setting parameters**
> - **Selecting an appropriate approach to your research**
> - **Identifying ethical considerations**
> - **Time management**
> - **Record keeping**
> - **Tutorial support**
> - **Avoiding the pitfalls**

The first point to remember is that your research project is unique to you. You will have your own ideas as to what you want to achieve and this chapter will offer you guidance on how to meet your aims. Your first task is to select your subject area. This can seem a simple thing to do, but often it becomes more complex when you begin to think it through in detail.

In helping to guide you through your personal planning and delivery of your work this chapter will refer you back to other chapters, prompting you to consider again the activities, checklists and 'Remember' points, and highlighting some of the problems which can be faced by researchers. Take note of the key terms in each chapter and refer to the glossary if you need to check their meanings.

As you work your way through this chapter, you will find examples following one particular student's research project. Some of these examples will be followed by activities for you to complete. This should help you with the planning of your own study. At the end of the chapter we will look at some of the pitfalls that can be experienced, especially by first-time researchers. You might want to refer to that section before you start planning, then return to it, using it as a prompt as your project progresses.

Choosing your subject area

There are a number of points to consider when selecting a subject area for your research project. These include:

- What interests you?
- How long do you have in which to complete your project?
- Does your project need to link to any particular aspect of a course of study?

You will need to keep your responses to each of these questions in mind as you explore ideas further.

Activity

Make a note of all the subjects that interest you. Include subject areas that:

■ link into your studies
■ fit in with future career plans
■ particularly interest you
■ would develop your understanding of something you consider to be important.

You might also want to consider a topic that no one you know of is aiming to research. This will help to make your research of greater interest to more of your peers. It will, however, mean that you will be less likely to have opportunities to share resources.

Use Figure 8.1 on page 104 (which, like most of the figures in this chapter, may be photocopied) to help you explore your ideas.

Having explored your initial ideas, using Figure 8.2 will help develop these thoughts further. Ask yourself:

■ How much does each subject on your list *really* interest you? Make a note of each in order of importance to you.
■ Why does it interest you? Make a note of your answers.
■ Does the subject in general appeal, or just one or two aspects of it?
■ How likely are you to get bored with the subject?
■ How easy will it be to obtain sources of information?

Share resources with other students where you can

Subject area	Links to your studies	Links to your career plans	Subject of particular importance to you	Specific area of interest to you	How easy will it be to share resources?

Figure 8.1   Choosing your subject area

Subject area	Order of preference 1 = highest	Why does it interest you? Note your reasons

This page may be photocopied.

Figure 8.2   Does a subject area really interest you?

In answering the questions above you will probably have narrowed your list of possibilities down. It is absolutely vital that your chosen subject will hold your interest for the duration of your study. It can be quite hard to maintain enthusiasm and commitment even when you are very interested in a subject, because of the workload and having to manage your time carefully, and perhaps having to adhere to tight deadlines. It is almost impossible to maintain sufficient motivation if you are bored with the subject. Discuss any concerns you have with your tutor.

Your next step is to take each subject area on your list in turn. Explore each subject by means of a **spidergraph**, to see how many lines of enquiry you could pursue. Figure 8.4 shows how one subject area can be developed logically through a series of stages.

Taking this approach has enabled Helen to see that there are many different areas that could be explored. If Helen chooses to continue with this subject, she would need to decide what her main focus (her aim) will be. She may decide that she wants to touch on all the ideas indicated, or she may decide to focus specifically on two or three. Whatever decision Helen makes, she will need to write a hypothesis or a research question, or identify an issue that she wants to explore specifically. The writing of these was discussed in Chapter 1. It is worth revisiting this to clarify your understanding.

Activity
Your own research proposal
Choose a subject area and explore it by using the spidergraphs as Helen has done, then answer the following questions:
■ How does your spidergraph compare to Helen's?
■ How does it fit in with your answers regarding your interests and any course requirements?
■ Will the subject keep your interest? Be honest. If not, you should carry on exploring alternative ideas.

If you think you have made the right decision regarding your subject area try the following activity.

Activity
For your chosen area of research:
1 Make a note of all sources of information you think will be available to you.
2 Decide which are likely to be the most useful for your chosen topic.
3 Consider how easily accessible these sources will be to you.
4 Consider how much time you can allow purely for your literature search.
Compare your outcomes to the checklist in Appendix B.

Have you used the Internet yet? Try visiting the Stanley Thornes website at www.thorneseducation.com. There is a range of information available which you may find helpful.

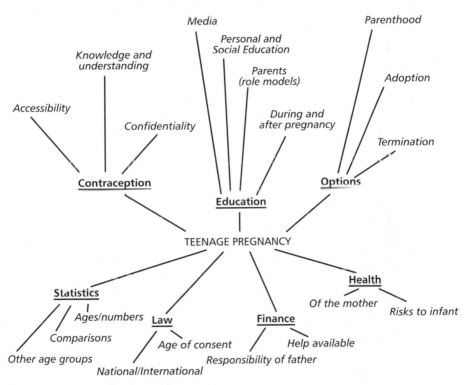

Figure 8.3   Example of a spidergraph

If you are happy with your plans so far, your next step is to consider writing your **aims** and **objectives**. If you are still unsure what subject to explore, arrange to speak to your tutor.

Writing your aims and objectives

The terms 'aim' and 'objective' are very similar in that they can both be defined as 'purpose'. There are, however, important differences. In the context of a research proposal, we can use the term 'aim' to refer to our overall purpose, whereas our 'objectives' are the specific things we intend to do to achieve our aim. Here we will use Helen and her interest in teenage pregnancy as an example.

AIMS

Helen's aims (her overall purpose) were set out as follows:

> The aim of this piece of research is to compare the number of teenage pregnancies in Britain, the USA and Scandinavia in the 1990s, noting whether this has changed in recent years. It will also consider levels of personal education within school programmes in each country and what support is available to young mothers.

OBJECTIVES

With these as her main aims, Helen set out her objectives (a breakdown of her aims into specific tasks) in the following way:

> By the end of this research project, I will have:
> 1 gathered and presented statistics on teenage pregnancies in each country
> 2 explained the personal education programmes included in schools in each country
> 3 made comparisons between the education programmes in each country, noting any links to pregnancy rates
> 4 identified any changes in pregnancy rates over recent years
> 5 discussed the support available to young mothers in each country.

You will see from these objectives that Helen has indicated how each aspect of the main aim will be explored. Objectives should not be seen as prescriptive or restrictive to the research, but rather as a guideline. Although it is expected that each objective is met during the research process, you may find that in reality some are met more fully than others.

Activities

Helen's proposal
Consider Helen's proposal set out above. Do you think that her objectives are likely to meet her aims? Why do you think this?

Being objective
The term objective also means 'without bias'. This was referred to in Chapter 1. Look again at Helen's proposal. How easy do you think Helen will find it to carry out an objective (unbiased) study on teenage pregnancy?

Your own research proposal
Write an overall aim and a set of objectives for your chosen subject. Remember to start your objectives with the statement
    By the end of this research project, I will have …
Discuss them with your tutor. Be ready to justify your intentions. Keep in mind the issue of objectivity. What difficulties with your proposal do you foresee? You might find Figure 8.4 useful.

The aim of this research project is to:

Objectives:

By the end of this research project, I will . . .

1

2

3

4

5

6

You need to set yourself enough objectives to cover your research fully, but ensure they are all of value.

This page may be photocopied.   © Stanley Thornes (Publishers) Ltd.

Figure 8.4   Writing your aims and objectives

It is important to refer back regularly to your aims and objectives. This will help you to keep focused. Research projects that 'lose their way' are often the result of the researcher not referring back regularly.

EVALUATING YOUR OBJECTIVES

An evaluation of your research will be asked of you as you reach the end of your project. In this you will usually be expected to refer to your aims and objectives, commenting on how well these have been met. Any objectives not met should be specifically discussed, giving an outline of why, in your view, this was the case. It is important that you show a clear understanding of the reasons. Although you are usually expected to achieve all of your objectives, you will not automatically be penalised during the assessment process if your explanation is well presented.

You may find that it is particularly appropriate to evaluate the decisions made at the onset of your project, when you will have set your aims and objectives in conjunction with setting your hypothesis, issue or research question.

SETTING OUT YOUR HYPOTHESIS, ISSUE OR RESEARCH QUESTION

Before attempting to set out a hypothesis, issue for discussion or research question for your own proposed subject area, you might find it useful to refer back to the discussion in Chapter 1.

When you have consolidated your understanding of the process, try the following activity.

Activity
Taking Helen's chosen subject, teenage pregnancy, choose *one* of the following:
1   Write a hypothesis.
2   Identify an issue.
3   Write a research question.
If you can, discuss these with another student. Decide between you how clearly your hypothesis, issue or research question is set out. Do you agree with each other's ideas? If not, explore why. What alternatives could you have used?

Now look at Helen's suggestions below. They include two hypotheses, two issues and two questions. How do your ideas compare with hers?

HELEN'S SUGGESTIONS

Hypotheses
1   Teenage pregnancy rates have increased as a result of greater social acceptance of single parenthood in society.

2 Increased information for teenagers about personal relationships would reduce pregnancy rates.

Issues for discussion
1 Changes in society's acceptance of teenage parenting: Have these had an effect on statistics?
2 The financial difficulties faced by teenage parents: What are the long-term effects on children?

Research questions
1 Is there a link between teenage pregnancy rates and levels of personal education in schools?
2 What are the main problems faced by teenage mothers today?

Activity
Evaluation of Helen's suggestions
Consider the following questions:
1 How feasible do you think Helen's suggestions would be?
2 Have you identified any significant difficulties she might face?
3 Do you think Helen would be trying to prove or disprove her hypotheses?
4 Are there any ethical issues Helen would need to consider? What would these be? (Chapter 5 considered ethical issues within research.)
5 Which of Helen's hypotheses, issues or questions would you choose? Why?

Your own research proposal
Write a hypothesis, an issue and a research question for the subject area (or areas) that you are considering. Again, discuss these with another student or your tutor. Evaluate your suggestions. How feasible do you think they would be? How easily understood are they? Be clear as to whether you would be trying to prove or disprove your hypothesis. Do others understand and agree with your suggestions? If not, explore why. What alternatives could you use? Have you or anyone else identified any significant difficulties that you might face? What ethical issues will you need to consider? Figure 8.5 may be of use to you.

Activity
Refer once again to Helen's ideas.
1 State which you would have chosen? Why?
2 State which you definitely would not have chosen? Why not?
Look at your reasons in conjunction with your suggestions for your own project. Do your ideas still seem logical and manageable? If so, you are ready to move on to the next stage of your project – setting the parameters of your study.

Subject area under consideration
Hypothesis
Issue
Question
Subject area under consideration
Hypothesis
Issue
Question

This page may be photocopied.   © *Stanley Thornes (Publishers) Ltd.*

Figure 8.5   Forming an hypothesis, issue or research question

Setting parameters

As explained in Chapter 3, setting the parameters of your work means deciding the scope of your work – how broadly or how narrowly you are going to explore the sources available to you. This will mainly be determined by your chosen subject area. Some subjects need to be explored in a broad context, referring to recent (or distant) history as well as current information. Other subjects need to be concentrated in the here and now. Some will benefit from comparisons with other countries and some will simply need a national, or even just a local, focus. Some subjects will require a great deal of input from other people (your participants), while some will only need to involve a few.

Having made your decision you will adjust your research accordingly. For example, if you are keeping your study in the here and now, you will not be referring back to statistics of ten years ago. Alternatively, if you are researching how something has changed (as Helen aimed to do), you will need both current and past statistics. If you need the views of many people you will probably produce questionnaires for a survey. If you only need one or two opinions you might consider carrying out some interviews. Refer back to the coverage of quantitative and qualitative research methods in Chapter 1, and make sure that you understand the difference between them.

Activity

Helen's proposal
Consider the following questions:
1 How would you describe the scope of Helen's work?
2 What parameters would you set yourself if you were Helen?
3 How far back would you research if you were researching teenage pregnancy?
4 How many participants might Helen need?
5 If you were Helen would you take a quantitative or a qualitative approach ? Why?
6 Might your approach be both quantitative and qualitative? If yes, in what ways?

Your own research proposal
Bearing in mind the questions above, try answering the following:
1 Do you consider your research proposal will be best addressed by a broad or a narrow scope? Why?
2 Will your research be quantitative or qualitative (or both)? Justify your decision both to yourself and to another student. Do you agree with each other?
3 What parameters could you set yourself? Make a list, including:
    a) How far back will you research?
    b) Will you make any comparisons? If yes, to what?
    c) How many participants do you consider you will need?
    d) What will be the impact on your project of any restrictions you set yourself?
Are you happy with your plans? If not, talk to your tutor. If you are, continue with your planning.

Selecting an appropriate approach to your research

Chapter 2 gave considerable coverage to the different primary research methods you could use. These included:

- interviews
- questionnaires
- action research
- observation
- case studies.

Secondary research methods were also set out. These included:

- using literature
- using technology
- statistics.

Activity
Helen's proposal
Consider the following information and then answer the questions below.

Helen chose to use questionnaires for her primary research, together with two interviews. Her questionnaires, aimed at teenagers both in secondary education and in further education, asked about the personal and social education (PSE) programmes they followed at school, and whether these had made them more aware of the level of parental responsibility and loss of freedom a pregnancy brings. Her interviews were with a young people's counsellor and an adviser from a pregnancy advisory clinic.

1. Which method of primary research would you have chosen?
2. Why would you have chosen it? Consider the alternatives. Why is your preferred method best (in your opinion)?

Helen would have been able to find supportive material for her study (secondary research) through published material on sociology and trends in family groupings. Magazines would have given her case studies to discuss. A variety of help and support organisations would also have been suitable sources for statistics and general information.

3. Where else might Helen have obtained suitable material?

Your own research proposal
You need to decide at this stage which method or methods you will use. Think about what you are aiming to achieve and how much time you have available. Weigh up the advantages and disadvantages of each method. Refer back to Chapter 2 for details. You may find it useful to explore triangulation (various methods, each backing up the findings of the others). Figures 8.6 and 8.7 may be helpful.

Three research methods each support each other, reinforcing validity and reliability.

method 1

subject area

method 2   method 3

Figure 8.6   Triangulation

What methods could you use for your chosen subject area?

Subject area	Interviews How many?	Questionnaires How many?	Action research	Observations How many?	Case studies

This page may be photocopied.

© Stanley Thornes (Publishers) Ltd.

Figure 8.7   Choosing an appropriate research method

- Interviews can be structured or unstructured.
- Interviews take up a considerable amount of time.
- Targeting the right people as participants is extremely important for both interviews and questionnaires.
- Questionnaires need careful wording. Refer back to Chapter 2 and the issue of open and closed questions.
- Do not use too many questions.
- Questionnaires can be a useful means of getting lots of opinions.
- Return rates with questionnaires are not always good.
- You should always carry out a 'pilot' survey to identify any ambiguities.
- With action research you will still be working with your participants afterwards. It is important not to upset them.
- Observations can be either participant or non-participant.
- Always gain appropriate permission in advance.
- Case studies can be particularly useful as a back-up to other methods.

Identifying ethical considerations

In Chapter 5 we explored ethical issues. You need now to apply these considerations to your own project.

Activity
Helen's proposal
Consider the following information and then answer the question below.

Helen knew that her subject area was a sensitive one. Two participants had become pregnant as teenagers and Helen needed to ensure that she indicated no judgement of their situation. Ethical issues Helen might also have faced in researching teenage pregnancies would include religious and cultural beliefs in relation to termination (abortion) and school policies on sex education within the PSE programmes.

- What other ethical issues (if any) should Helen be aware of?

Your own research proposal
As you prepare your research you will need to ask yourself the following questions:
1 Who might be involved in your research?
2 From where will you need to obtain your permission for involving them?
3 What particularly sensitive issues (if any) will you need to be aware of?
4 What are the rights of the individuals involved?
5 How important are confidentiality and anonymity within your research?
Complete Figure 8.8 to clarify the issues within your chosen subject area.

What ethical issues might you need to consider?

Subject area	Is this a sensitive subject?	In what way is it sensitive?	How might it negatively affect your participants?	How might it restrict your research?

This page may be photocopied.   © Stanley Thornes (Publishers) Ltd.

Figure 8.8   Ethical issues in research

Time management

Management of your time is important. You will need to set out a time plan, and will probably need to submit your plan with your completed project. Be realistic about what you are going to be able to achieve in a given amount of time. If you set yourself unrealistic targets and cannot meet them you will always feel that you are behind with your work. This is a very demoralising way to approach something. Reschedule your time plan if necessary. This will help you regain control of your time management. Some weeks you will have more time available to you than others. Use that time well. Write off for information sooner rather than later, as it often takes quite a while for material to be returned to you. It is important to always enclose a stamped addressed envelope. This is good manners (why should the charity or organisation pay for your postage!), and it often gets you a quicker and better response. Some organisations need payment to cover the materials they send out. Whenever possible, send a donation to cover costs, particularly to charities.

Figures 8.9 to 8.11 show an example of a time plan at different stages of completion. Figure 8.9 is a blank form for you to fill in. Figure 8.10 shows what your initial time plan might look like. Figure 8.11 shows the same plan with the addition of the date each action was completed, and your own brief comments, giving a 'running commentary' on how your work is progressing. Always check to see whether there is a set requirement by your college or school regarding the format of your written plans.

This style of planning will enable both you and your tutor to see how well you have managed your time, as you are indicating your intended deadlines as well as the actual dates you have achieved each stage.

When you have looked at the example, evaluate the planning style. How does it compare with your usual way of working? Do you have an alternative approach that works well for you? Check with your tutor whether it is acceptable. There is no set style of planning, but you do need to show your research process clearly. Your plans also need to reflect the appropriate amount of time allowed for the completion of your research project. For a very long research period it might be more appropriate to write your plans month by month. Again, check this with your tutor.

Throughout your research, keep in regular touch with your tutor. They are there to help and advise you.

Record keeping

In Chapter 3 we discussed how good record keeping helps you to manage your time, particularly in avoiding the need to re-locate useful material. It also enables you to clearly reference your sources, avoiding plagiarism. As you plan your project, it is advisable to categorise your sources, noting which aspect of your research each source will be of benefit to.

Action to be taken	By when?	Help/information needed	Date completed	Any comments?

This page may be photocopied.

Figure 8.9   Time plan: blank form

Action to be taken	By when?	Help/information needed	Date completed	Any comments?
Write aims & obj's & set my hypothesis	20.4	Check with tutor		
Spidergraph	20.4	My own thoughts		
Spidergraph	27.4	Extended using library resources		
Write draft letters to:	1.5	Family planning centre Brook Street Bureau Health Education Council Two local schools (What advice is given to young people?)		
Literature search	4.5	Explore college library further – books (note down useful resources)		
Literature search	11.5	– magazines & journals (note down useful resources)		
Consider my research methodology	16.5	Read through class notes & look at research methods books		
Tutorial	18.5	Ask tutor about research methods I am considering Take along copies of letters to be checked		
Send off letters	20.5	W/P letters & post		

Figure 8.10   Time plan filled in by student: stage 1

Action to be taken	By when?	Help/information needed	Date completed	Any comments?
Write aims & obj's & set my hypothesis	20.4	Check with tutor	20.4	Overall aim is O.K. I need to re-look at obj's 4, 5 & 6
Spidergraph	20.4	My own thoughts	20.4	A good start
Spidergraph	27.4	Extend using library resources	27.4	Have now got an extensive 'spider' to work from
Write draft letters to:	1.5	Family planning centre Brooke Street Bureau Health Education Council Two local schools (What advice is given to young people?)	30.4	Need to get my letters checked. Tutorial is on 18.5
Literature search	4.5	Explore college library further – books (note down useful resources)	4.5	4 good books & 3 possibilities Details noted
Literature search	11.5	– magazines & journals (note down useful resources)	11.5	Nothing as yet Need to get teen' mags
Consider my research methodology	16.5	Read through class notes & look at research methods books	16.5	May interview a couple of teenage mothers
Tutorial	18.5	Ask tutor about research methods I am considering Take along copies of letters to be checked		
Send off letters	20.5	W/P letters & post		

Figure 8.11   Time plan: stage 2, with added comments

MAKING NOTES FOR YOUR CHOSEN STUDY

Once you have decided on your aims and objectives, and have set your parameters, your next step is to explore your chosen subject area in some depth and obtain a range of sources of information. At this stage you will need to make a note of the following:

1 the categories or topics you intend to use (each one on a separate sheet)
2 appropriate subheadings (on each sheet) at intervals down the page
3 the information sources you have, under each subheadings
4 the sources of information you still need to locate (you may find this easier if you use a separate sheet of paper).

This process can form a cycle of literature research, whereby each time you complete the cycle you identify areas needing further research, until you feel that your literature search is complete (see Figure 8.12)

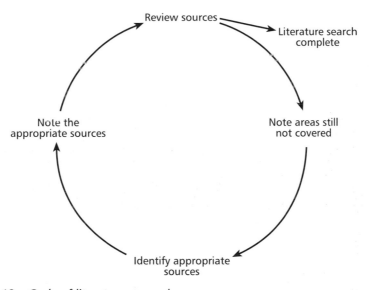

Figure 8.12   Cycle of literature research

Tutorial support

Your tutor is there to help you. You will most likely have tutorials on a regular basis. Tutors are likely to have a broad knowledge and understanding of many subjects, although they will not guarantee to be an authority on your particular subject. However, they will almost certainly be able to point you in the direction of someone who is and also be able to recommend relevant sources of information. It is up to you to make good use of your tutorials by going to them fully prepared.

Your tutor will usually be very willing to help you

CHECKLIST FOR GETTING THE BEST OUT OF YOUR TUTORIALS

- Keep a notebook for writing down any questions you have. Make a note of them as soon as they arise.
- Take your notebook with you.
- Check your aims and objectives with your tutor. Are they considered appropriate?
- Outline the parameters you intend to set for yourself. Be able to justify them.
- Explain which method or methods of primary research you intend to use. Be ready to justify this.
- Consider the ethical issues raised by your subject.
- Demonstrate your understanding of ethics by raising the issues you have identified. Try to have suggestions ready for dealing with the issues you have identified.
- Be ready to outline the rights of your participants to show your understanding.
- Discuss any implications of these rights for decisions you have made.
- Ask for guidance, if you need it, regarding secondary sources of information.

You may find it helpful to use the example of a blank form for tutorial notes given in Figure 8.13. Figure 8.14 shows a completed set of notes.

REMEMBER

Your tutor cannot answer your questions unless you have actually asked them.

POSITIVE CRITICISM

Your tutor will offer positive criticism as well as advice. Positive criticism is a form of appraisal or assessment. It is intended to help you evaluate your research whilst

Name: Name of tutor:

Date of tutorial: Location:

_____

I need to take the following with me:

Points for discussion:

Questions:

Date of next tutorial:

This page may be photocopied.   © *Stanley Thornes (Publishers) Ltd.*

Figure 8.13   Reminder notes for tutorials: blank form

Name: A. Student   Name of tutor: M. Y. Tutor

Date of tutorial: Location:

_____

I need to take the following with me:

Copy of my aims and objectives

Rough draft letter to local nursery manager

Examples of resources gathered to date

Points for discussion:

Idea for my hypothesis

The layout and content of my letter

Methods I could use - Interviews
                     - Questionnaires

Questions:

Is it OK to contact my local MP for a political view?

How do I refer to the nursery without naming it?

How soon should I do my survey or interviews?

Date of next tutorial:

Figure 8.14   Reminder notes for tutorials: completed example

it is in progress. Take the comments given in the spirit they are intended. They are aimed at helping you develop your research skills in general as well as within this current piece of work. Your research project is part of your learning process. Therefore you will need to reflect on comments made, and use them to review what you do next as part of that learning process. For some education programmes this is a mandatory part of the course.

Avoiding the pitfalls

It is always useful to learn from the mistakes of others, and so the last part of this chapter is given over to identifying points in the research process where new researchers can easily go wrong.

The three most common errors made by first-time researchers are as follows:
- unnecessary re-reading of material that has already been discarded
- inadequate record keeping
- failing to acknowledge sources when material has been reworked.

The simple guidelines below will help you to avoid these pitfalls. We will look at each of them in turn.

UNNECESSARY RE-READING OF MATERIAL THAT HAS ALREADY BEEN DISCARDED

Re-reading material is often necessary, and indeed it is good practice for us to consolidate our understanding of what a writer is saying. This is a very positive reason for returning to a book or journal. It is the re-reading of material unnecessarily that needs to be avoided. This can occur for two main reasons. The first is that we have failed to make a note of a book or journal that is not going to be of any use to us. We are likely to gravitate towards such books again as we scan our libraries and bookshops on future occasions. This happens because when we are focused on a particular topic, relevant titles of books 'jump out' at us, encouraging us to scan their pages. We can avoid wasting valuable time in this manner by carrying out the simple task of keeping clear records, as already discussed.

The second reason is that we have taken down insufficient details of a source which we later decide we want to refer to within our writing. Our record keeping is inadequate if it does not include all the details we might need.

INADEQUATE RECORD KEEPING

A frequent mistake made by first-time researchers is to forget to note the page number along with other details, such as title, author, and so on. This simple error can cause hours of frustration as you strive to find again the appropriate page in a particular book in order to use relevant information or an ideal quote. This can be prevented by using the guidance previously outlined. Refer back to Chapter 4 for guidance on referencing and the writing out of your bibliography.

FAILING TO ACKNOWLEDGE SOURCES WHEN MATERIAL HAS BEEN REWORKED

Plagiarism has been discussed in Chapter 4 and mentioned at other times too. Be sure that you are clear about your responsibilities with regard to referencing and acknowledging sources. At times you may read and want to use information from another source, without actually quoting from it. You need always to be clear when your written text is your own and when it is the reworked writing of somebody else.

When possible, put things into your own words. Your opinions are important and will be valued by the readers of your project. If a passage of your text is a rewording of material from another source you must make this clear. You can do this by giving the reference after the passage, for example:

Source of reading: Bloggs (1996, p. 75)

Assuming that you have now completed your literature search and have carried out both your primary and your secondary research, you will be ready to consider the presentation of your research project. This is covered in Chapter 9.

Chapter summary

- Planning logically is important and will help you manage your time.
- Writing aims and objectives gives you a set of guidelines to refer back to.
- A hypothesis, issue or research question is needed to give your work a focus.
- It is important to set yourself parameters within which you will work.
- It is important that you select appropriate research methods for your subject.
- Ethical considerations should always be considered.
- Keeping detailed records of the research process may help you later on.
- Use the tutorial support available to you well.

KEY TERMS

You should now understand the following words and phrases. If you do not, go back through the chapter and review them.

Spidergraph   Objective
Aim

---

9 PRESENTING YOUR RESEARCH

> ## This chapter covers:
> - **Dividing your project into sections**
> - **Approaching each section of the project**
> - **Proofreading**
> - **Preparing for an oral presentation**

By the time you reach this stage of your project you will already have done all the hard work and now all you need is to set it out ready for presentation and assessment. However, good presentation is critical, and even the best research findings will be useless if others cannot access and understand your work. It is quite possible that you may have to present your findings to a group, and this chapter covers both written and oral presentation of your research.

Dividing your project into sections

As with all assignments, you need to identify clearly your introduction and your conclusions. These naturally fall at the beginning and end of the main body of your work. For a research project, you will be expected to divide up your work still further. The following categories are commonly used in written presentations:
- **Abstract**
- Introduction
- **Methodology**
- Presentation of data
- Main text
- Conclusion and any recommendations
- Evaluation
- Bibliography
- **Appendices**.

These are discussed in turn in 'Approaching each section of the project' below.

Your project should follow a logical sequence, taking the reader through the different stages of your research. You are likely to be assessed on your planning and on your time management (this will be evidenced by your plans and evaluation as well as by the quality of your overall research). Your plans should indicate how you have thought ahead, managed your time well and taken into consideration how long each stage of your project will take. An example of time planning is given in Chapter 8.

You will also be assessed on the way in which you approached your research (your chosen methods, the scope of your work and the justifications for your choices), together with how well you have combined primary and secondary methods. Your overall conclusions and recommendations, together with your evaluation, will add to the evidence of your understanding of the subject studied and the outcomes presented. These should therefore not be considered as 'additional extras'. They are important evidence towards your overall grade.

In addition to the sections listed above, your project will need to start with a title page and a contents page.

TITLE PAGE

This should include the title of your research project, your name, your tutor's name, and the date. If your project has a course title ('Research Project', 'Community Assignment', 'Module 8', 'Dissertation', and so on) this should also be clearly set out. Figure 9.1 is an example of a title page.

CONTENTS PAGE

This clearly lists each section of your project, giving the number of the first page of each section. Figure 9.2 shows a contents page. The page numbers here are used purely as an example. The length of your work will be determined by a number of factors, including:

- the course guidelines
- the set word length (if you have been given one)
- the size of the typeface you have used (size 14 is usually the largest to be accepted)
- whether your text is single or double spaced (double spaced is usually preferred, as this allows room for pencilled comments)
- how you have set out your paragraphs (e.g. with or without an extra space between each one)
- the number of illustrations you have included
- any dividing pages, if you have chosen to use them.

Approaching each section of the project

ABSTRACT

An abstract is a brief summary of the whole project. It states the aims, the research methods used, and the conclusions drawn. This gives an 'at a glance' summary of your work. Figure 9.3 is an example of an abstract.

This is an aspect of presentation which is usually only required for a Level 4 course. If you are completing research for part of a Level 3 course such as Nursery Nursing or a GNVQ it will probably not be required. Your tutor will be able to confirm this.

Your Title page may look like this:

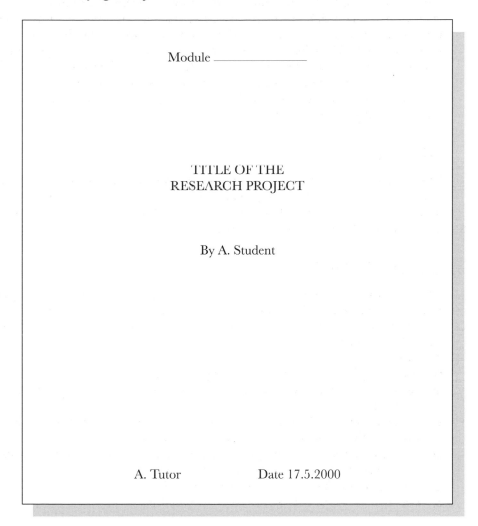

Figure 9.1   Example of title page

INTRODUCTION

This is largely self-explanatory. You introduce your subject area by setting out your aims and objectives, together with the parameters you have decided upon. You would not usually include discussion here. Whilst you need to know approximately how you will introduce your work, it is often better to write out your introduction in rough, leaving the writing of the final version until last. In taking this approach you will ensure that you introduce exactly what you have written and not just what you intended to write earlier on. Regularly referring back to your aims and objectives should keep you focused.

Contents

v

Figure 9.2   Example of contents page

THE IMPORTANCE OF MULTICULTURAL AWARENESS WITHIN THE PRE-SCHOOL SETTING

BY JAYNE OLPIN

(April 1999)

This assignment examines the anti-discriminatory framework and its importance within early years work. It considers the views of early years workers and parents using pre-school provision as to how important multicultural awareness is within that setting. The assignment focuses on two workplaces within the pre-school provision used, workplace A and workplace B.

The research methods used in the assignment are three small-scale questionnaires and a small piece of action research.

The provision of resources is examined, and there follows a discussion of how these resources can be better used within the curriculum in order to remove tokenism.

The report goes on to examine the consequences of not implementing an anti-discriminatory framework, including racism and discrimination.

The report concludes that there is scope for improvement in the way the curriculum is planned and delivered in order to promote multicultural awareness within the workplace.

Source: Jayne Olpin

The above abstract sets out what the researcher was aiming for in her research. This is followed by a description of her methods of research – three small-scale questionnaires and a piece of action research. The conclusion, drawn from the findings of the research, is briefly stated at the end.

The abstract gives the reader a brief 'overview' of the intentions of the research, the primary research process and the conclusions drawn by the researcher.

Figure 9.3   Example of an abstract. An abstract is concise and will often take up less than one side of A4 paper

METHODOLOGY

In this section you are expected to describe and justify your choice of research methods. You need to state whether your study has been quantitative or qualitative, or a combination of the two. You need to explain what primary research is and what methods of primary research you have used. It is important that you also outline the secondary methods you have used, justifying each, and giving a brief explanation of why alternative methods were not chosen. For example, why did you elect to carry out six interviews rather than hand out questionnaires? What was the benefit of one method over the other? It is important that you show your understanding of research methodology in general. Explain any ethical considerations you may have had, demonstrating your awareness of their importance. State why you consider your work to be valid and how your chosen methods have given you reliable data. Refer back to Chapter 2 and try to include some discussion of research methods you have not used, explaining why. This might be because of personal choice, or it might be that the methods not used would have been unsuitable for the subject area or type of study you were carrying out.

PRESENTATION OF DATA

If you have produced graphs, charts, diagrams or tables of information taken from your primary research (your interviews, questionnaires, and so on), this is where you will present them. Database and spreadsheet programmes will facilitate this task if you can use them and have access to them. Some schools and colleges will have specific statistics packages that you can use too. Remember that your graphs, charts, and so on (your data) need to be placed in the correct order, that is the order in which they are referred to in the text. They must be clearly numbered, and an explanation of what they show needs to be given wherever necessary. Refer back to Chapter 7 to consolidate your understanding of these methods of presentation. Make sure that you cross-reference your data to your written text. This means stating on which page further discussion of each item can be found. You also need to include cross-references in your written text to your data (e.g. 'See Table 5').

MAIN TEXT

This will be the largest section of your project. It is here that you will discuss your work as a whole. You will describe any problems experienced, make reference to your aims and objectives, and refer to your many sources of information. You will use discussion and debate throughout. It is important that you make clear your own views. As you discuss you will make reference to the thoughts, opinions and findings of others, making relevant quotations, and you will ensure that you have included full details of these sources.

CONCLUSION AND ANY RECOMMENDATIONS

In this section there should be no new information added. Your conclusions should be drawn from what has already been presented and discussed. If you are making recommendations for future research, or perhaps even what the Government or your local authority should (in your opinion) do, this is where you will set them out. You should make specific reference to your hypothesis, issue or research question, and to your aims, noting whether your aims have been met.

EVALUATION

At this point you will evaluate both the outcomes of your research and how successfully you have carried it out. Your evaluation should demonstrate clearly that you have reflected on your work. Take an honest look at your research process. How well did your planning and time management go? What would you change for future projects? Has any decision that you have made altered the outcomes of your work? Was this a positive or a negative consequence? In what way?

Chapter 10 encourages you to reflect on the whole research process, including the presentation of your work, both orally and in writing. Evaluation is an important skill which you are encouraged to consider how well you have developed.

BIBLIOGRAPHY

Your bibliography will list all the books, journals and other sources that you have used and made reference to. You may want to add a list of other sources used purely for background reading. Check with your tutor whether these should be set out separately. If so, you would have a section headed 'Bibliography' and a section below it headed 'Other sources of reference'. This will clearly differentiate between the sources you have directly used and those that have been used in a more indirect manner. If you are still unsure of referencing techniques refer back to Chapter 4 for guidance.

APPENDICES

An appendix is an 'add on' or a supplement to your work. These should be used sparingly. The ideal time to use an appendix is when you want to include a copy of a blank questionnaire or set of interview prompts to illustrate to the reader what initiated your data. An appendix should not simply be copies of information sources. Anything presented as an appendix should be referred to within your study, usually in either the presentation of data section or in the main text. If an appendix is not discussed or referred to during the presentation of your project it should not be included.

Proofreading

Proofreading is the systematic reading through of the 'finished' product. It enables you to check grammar, spellings and clarity. It is important that you always proofread your work. Ideally this should be before you have written (or printed out) your final copy, to avoid wastage. It can also be useful to ask another person to read it through too, giving you feedback on the clarity and flow of your text.

Your bibliography will list all the books and journals that you have used

Remember to use a dictionary and then the spell-check facility on your computer if you have it. Also, remember that the spell-check will not identify where you have used an inappropriate word, for example 'their' instead of 'there'. Be aware that many spell-check programmes are American, and therefore some spellings will also be different. Time for proofreading should be included in your planning. The overall quality of your work can be badly let down by spelling and grammatical errors.

REMEMBER

Following the various stages set out within this book will help you to increase your understanding of research methods and enable you to enjoy successfully producing your first piece of research.

Preparing for an oral presentation

Presenting the outcomes of your research orally also needs to be given specific planning time. You need to be thinking not only of the clarity of your delivery through voice levels and diction, but also of the visual impact you are making on your audience.

Many programmes of study now include a mandatory oral presentation as part of the research component. You will be assessed on this as well as on your written materials. You may be asked to give your presentation to a large group, but most likely you will be asked to give it to a small number of your fellow students. In either situation you will need to consider how best you can present your work and allow time to prepare for it fully.

PLANNING AN ORAL PRESENTATION

You will normally be told in advance how many people you will be presenting your work to, and how long your presentation is expected to last. If you have not been told, ask your tutor. This information is usually a guideline, and is not always strictly adhered to. A slightly short, but clear, interesting presentation which demonstrates preparation, knowledge and understanding of the subject, together with enthusiasm, will be assessed more highly than a long-winded presentation demonstrating little preparation or forethought.

You also need to know where your presentation will be held. This will help you decide how loud you need to speak, where you will position yourself and how far away visual resources will be from your audience.

You need to allow time to prepare each aspect of a presentation. Write this into your time plan early on in your studies. Visual resources often take longer to prepare than anticipated. Consider the points set out in the following sections.

BENEFITS OF AN ORAL PRESENTATION

An oral presentation should not be seen as an 'add-on'. It is an integral part of the research process, and an important skill. Oral presentations promote personal development in many different ways. Giving a presentation helps to build self-confidence. It allows the researcher to demonstrate their skills to their peers. Quiet members of a group often surprise their peers with their ability to give a presentation that is clear and confident, in addition to being well thought out. This can have the effect of bringing individuals closer together through a mutual understanding of the need for support and the sharing of new ideas. Oral presentations may seem daunting, but people often surprise themselves by how well they manage.

VISUAL RESOURCES

An oral presentation needs a focus. This is usually of a visual nature. There are many different resources you can use. You will almost certainly include some of the following:

- overhead projector transparencies
- audio-visual resources (tape recorders, videos, slides)
- tables, charts and graphs
- handouts.

You will also need to consider how to handle questions from your audience.

Activity
Think of any other visual or audio resources that might be relevant to your particular research topic. Make a note of them and then consider how they might enhance your oral presentation. Give careful consideration to the amount of preparation time they will need.

Overhead projector (OHP) transparencies

These useful transparencies give you the opportunity to exhibit information to the whole group at the same time. They also avoid the need for anyone to be looking down at a handout or sheet of statistics whilst you are talking. This encourages your audience to listen more carefully and to think about your subject area.

Transparencies need to be written clearly or typed in a large font size (16 is a useful size for small group presentations; a larger size should be used for larger groups). If you need to hand-write your transparencies, OHP pens are available in either permanent or erasable ink. If your tutor is providing resources for you, you will usually be expected to use erasable ink to allow the transparencies to be reused (they are an expensive resource). You can always take a photocopy of each transparency before you return them, to include with your written materials. OHP pens are available in many colours. The use of different colours helps to break text up into sections. This can be easier for the audience to read. Be careful as you handle them, as some inks can smudge quite easily.

It is important that there is not too much information on a transparency, as this can detract from what you are saying. Transparencies should be used to back up your oral presentation, ideally with bullet or numbered points (see Figure 9.5). They should not be a complete written version of what you are saying. The following is a useful checklist for successful transparencies.

- Clarity of typing or writing is vital.
- The size of type or writing needs to be suitable for the size of your group.
- Use different colours to break up the text.
- Restrict the amount of information on any one sheet.
- Include only the main points of what you are saying, or use the transparency to present supporting material.

PowerPoint

Microsoft's PowerPoint is a software presentation tool, akin to a 'slide show'. It enables you to present your visual material directly from a computer, replacing overhead projector transparencies or photographic slides. With PowerPoint you can move text and merge images during your oral presentation, eliminating the need to change transparencies, refer to diagrams on posters, and so on. It can be set up to run automatically, or under user control (for example, the user clicks on a mouse button to activate the next presentation slide). For this to be a successful means of presentation, a good understanding of how to use PowerPoint is important, and reliable equipment is crucial, as a technological problem at the last moment could mean an end to your presentation. This facility is increasingly available in colleges, but it is less likely to be available in schools. Ask your tutor or librarian about its availability to you.

Audio-visual resources

You may feel it is appropriate to use a short piece of video footage within your presentation. The relevance of anything you show needs to be very clear to your audience. It needs to add something to your talk to be of value, and should not be used if you could explain its content just as effectively without it. It is important

OHP transparencies should be clear and concise. Allow plenty of space between points.

<u>Research subject area</u>

1. _____

2. _____

3. _____

4. _____

5. _____

6. _____

Figure 9.4   Example of an overhead projector transparency, using numbered points for clarity

that video equipment is set up in advance and is ready for use. This includes finding the right place in the footage so that you do not keep your audience waiting while you search for it.

The same guidelines apply to slides and to audio tapes. Audio tapes will need to be very clear for them to be of any use within a presentation.

Before you use any audio-visual material in a presentation you need to be sure that you are not breaching any ethical agreements of confidentiality or anonymity. Always be certain that you have permission to use the material. The following is a useful checklist for successful audio-visual resources.

- Audio-visual resources need to be directly relevant.
- They should add something specific to your presentation.
- They should be set up, ready for use.
- They should be of good quality. This is particularly important with audio tapes.
- Be sure you have permission to use them.
- Never breech ethical agreements.

Tables, charts and graphs

If you need to include tables, charts or graphs within your presentation, they are best set out on an OHP transparency (as discussed above). You might like to back this up further by the use of a handout, to be distributed at the end of your presentation. This will enable your audience to continue to consider the content of your presentation at a later time.

Handouts

A handout is a sheet of information relevant to what you have been presenting. Handouts can be a useful way of consolidating the understanding of those you are talking to, by giving them material to read again at a later time. Handouts need to be clear and inviting to read (not too crowded with information) and directly relevant. It is important that handouts are given out after you have completed your oral presentation, as giving them out beforehand could distract your audience, who might be tempted to read them through rather than listen to what you have to say. A handout should back up the information you present orally, and offer opportunity to extend it further. Always ensure that you have enough for all those present, as well as a copy for your tutor. Remember to keep a copy within your written presentation too.

Activity

Look at the examples of handouts in Figures 9.6 to 9.9.
- Are they clear?
- What do you like about them?
- Is there anything you do not like about them?
- Is all the information current?
- Could any of the handouts be used as OHP transparencies? Which ones?
- Discuss your thoughts with another student. How do your views compare?

MULTIPLE BIRTHS

Statistics (1988) – England

Sets of twins	7,452
Sets of triplets	157
Sets of quadruplets	12
Sets of quintuplets	1

Types of twins
Monozygotic (MZ)
Identical boys/identical girls = 1/3 of all twins

Dizygotic (DZ)
Non-identical boys/non-identical girls = 2/3 of all twins
Boy/girl twins (sometimes known as fraternal twins)

Triplets and more
These may be any combination, depending on whether one egg was split (MZ), or three or more eggs were fertilized at the same time (DZ).

Approximately one in every forty-eight children will be a twin or multiple.

Figure 9.5   Example of a handout: Multiple births

Motor Skills			
Age	Locomotor skills	Non-locomotor skills	Manipulative skills
1 month	Stepping reflex	Lifts head; visually follows slowly moving objects	Holds object if placed in hand
2–3 months		Briefly keeps head up if held in sitting position	Begins to swipe at objects within visual range
4–6 months	Sits up with some support	Holds head erect in sitting position	Reaches for and grasps toys
7–9 months	Sits without support; rolls over in prone; crawls		Transfers objects from one hand to the other
10–12 months	Crawls; walks, grasping furniture, then without help	Squats and stoops	Some sign of hand preference; grasps a spoon across palm but poor aim of food to mouth
13–18 months	Walks backwards and sideways	Rolls ball to adult	Stacks 2 blocks; puts objects into small containers and dumps them
18–24 months	Runs (20); walks well; climbs stairs – both feet to a step	Pushes and pulls boxes or wheeled toys; unscrews lid on a jar	Shows clear hand preference. Stacks 4–6 blocks. Turns pages 1 at a time. Picks things up, keeping balance.
2–3 years	Runs easily; climbs up and down from furniture unaided	Hauls and shoves big toys around obstacles	Picks up small objects; throws small ball forward while standing
3–4 years	Walks upstairs one foot per step; skips on both feet; walks on tiptoe	Pedals and steers a tricycle; walks in any direction pulling a big toy	Catches large ball between outstretched arms; cuts paper with scissors; holds pencil between thumb and first 2 fingers
4–5 years	Walks up and down stairs, one foot per stair. Stands, runs and walks well on tiptoe		Strikes balls with bat; kicks and catches ball; threads bead, but not needle. Grasps pencil maturely
5–6 years	Skips on alternate feet; walks a thin line; slides and swings		Plays ball games quite well. Threads needles; can sew a stitch
7–8 years	Skips 12+ times	Rides 2-wheeler bike, short distances	Writes letters
8+ years	Skips freely	Rides bike easily	

Source: Helen Bee, 6th edition

Figure 9.6   Example of a handout: Motor Skills

The Apgar Score			
Aspects of Infants observed	**0**	**1**	**2**
Heart rate	Absent	<100/min	>100/min
Respiratory rate	No breathing	Weak cry and shallow breathing	Good, strong cry and regular breathing
Muscle tone	Flaccid	Some flexion of extremities	Well flexed
Response to stimulation of feet	None	Some motion	Crying
Colour	Blue; pale	Body colour normal with blue extremities	Normal colour

Figure 9.7   Example of a handout: The Apgar score

The following is a useful checklist for successful handouts.
- Handouts should be clear and inviting to read.
- They should back up what you are saying in your oral presentation.
- They should not be too crowded.
- Always give handouts out after your presentation.
- Ensure that you have enough copies to go round.

HANDLING QUESTIONS FROM YOUR AUDIENCE

Following an oral presentation, it is usual to offer the chance for the audience to ask questions. You need to think about this beforehand. Consider what questions you might ask, if you were in the audience for your own oral presentation. Remember that many of those listening will not be familiar with the subject beforehand.

As you plan your oral presentation think of additional material that might interest people, but cannot be included within your limited time allocation. You might find it helpful to have additional notes to hand to prompt you when questions are asked. It is also a good idea to have additional resources and copies of useful information available.

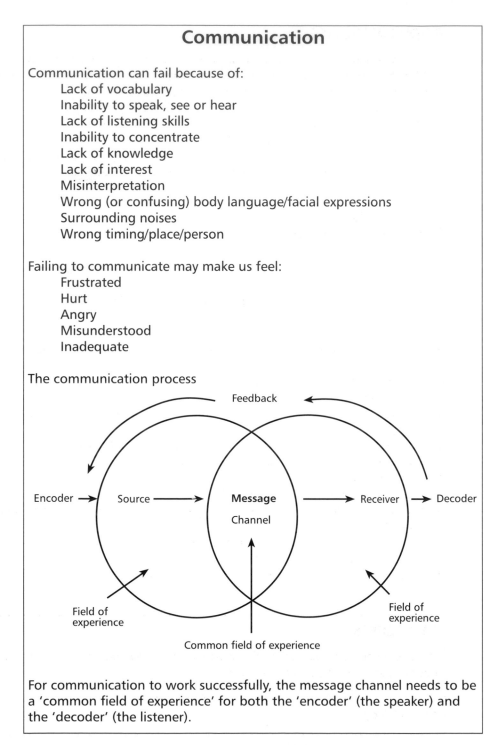

Communication

Communication can fail because of:
> Lack of vocabulary
> Inability to speak, see or hear
> Lack of listening skills
> Inability to concentrate
> Lack of knowledge
> Lack of interest
> Misinterpretation
> Wrong (or confusing) body language/facial expressions
> Surrounding noises
> Wrong timing/place/person

Failing to communicate may make us feel:
> Frustrated
> Hurt
> Angry
> Misunderstood
> Inadequate

The communication process

Feedback

Encoder → Source → **Message** → Receiver → Decoder

Channel

Field of experience

Common field of experience

Field of experience

For communication to work successfully, the message channel needs to be a 'common field of experience' for both the 'encoder' (the speaker) and the 'decoder' (the listener).

Figure 9.8   Example of a handout: Communication

BODY LANGUAGE

Although you are likely to feel a bit apprehensive when giving an oral presentation for the first time you need to be aware of your body language and voice level. Most importantly you need to make eye contact with your audience in order to 'engage' them in your presentation. Speak as clearly as you can. Try to speak to the back of the room, keeping your head up, rather than speaking into your notes, as your voice will become muffled and lost.

Turning your head or body to address all those listening will help to keep them all involved. Remember that they too will be giving a presentation and will feel just as you do.

Chapter summary

- Adequate time needs to be allocated for planning both written and oral presentations.
- The written presentation of your work needs to be divided into relevant sections.
- Course guidelines (if appropriate) need to be adhered to.
- You will normally be expected to show understanding of research methods in general.
- All graphically presented data need to be numbered, captioned and discussed in your main text.
- Your main text should include discussion, your own views and the analysis of your primary research.
- Your conclusion should be drawn from what has been discussed.
- It is important to include an evaluation of your research.
- A bibliography is needed.
- Appendices should be used sparingly.
- Your work should always be proofread, preferably by another person as well as yourself.
- Oral presentations benefit from the use of visual resources.
- Body language and eye contact are important.
- Be prepared to answer questions from your audience.

KEY TERMS

You should now understand the following words and phrases. If you do not, go back through the chapter and review them.

Abstract   Appendix
Methodology

---

10 *APPLYING YOUR RESEARCH SKILLS*

> **This chapter covers:**
> ■ **Evaluating the success of your project**
> ■ **Identifying what you have learnt**
> ■ **Evaluating your own learning**
> ■ **Using your skills**

Evaluation is an important skill that we each need to develop. Evaluation in the context of a research project incorporates your plans, your actions, and both the written and oral presentations of your work. As you carry out your evaluation you will identify the strengths and weaknesses, the successes and failures, of what you have achieved. You will also make a judgement as to what value it will be to you in the future. In the context of research you will have asked yourself whether your work is valid, reliable and representative. Your answers to these questions will have given you a judgement as to the success of your project overall.

Evaluating your skills in a more general sense, and deciding how those skills will be of value to you in the future, takes a little more exploration. This chapter will help you to identify how the process involved in completing your research project has enabled you to use and develop a variety of skills which will hopefully continue to be of value to you. Much of this chapter is set out as questions. Answer them as honestly as you can. If possible, discuss the outcomes in your group.

Evaluating the success of your project

As you consider your research project, ask yourself the following questions:
1 Were your aims and objectives clear?
2 Were they fully met?
3 If not, can you identify why this was the case?
4 If you set a hypothesis, was it proved or disproved?
5 If you set yourself a research question, was it answered?
6 Were the parameters you set yourself appropriate? How do you justify this?
7 How successful was your primary research?
8 Would an alternative method have been better?
9 How well did you interact with participants involved with your primary research?
10 How many new experiences did you have in carrying out and presenting your work?

11 Was your literature base sufficient for the scope of your project?

12 Did you identify all the ethical issues that you should have?

13 How well did you present your data?

14 How well did you discuss it? Were you analytical, or simply descriptive?

15 Were you able to draw conclusions?

16 How reliable do you consider your outcomes to be? How can you justify this?

17 What technology did you use during your research? What aspect of this was new to you?

18 Does your work meet the module requirements?

19 How good is the written presentation of your work? Could it have been improved?

20 How well written is your work? Did you check your spellings and grammar?

21 Is your work set out in a logical order?

22 How well does your work flow?

23 How well did you manage your time?

24 Does your work reflect the length of time allocated to complete it?

25 Do you think your work has earned you a pass grade? Or higher? Why?

Having reflected on your actual project, it will now be helpful to break it down into different skill areas, and consider what you have learnt, and its value to you. The four skill areas identified here are:

- oral skills
- written skills
- information technology skills
- numerical skills.

Identifying what you have learnt

ORAL SKILLS

For most students, giving an oral presentation following a research project is a first-time experience. This will have involved presenting information clearly to a small group, answering their questions and describing the overall process that the research project has taken. Oral skills will also have been needed during primary research to carry out

- interviews
- phone calls
- discussion.

Interviews

If you have used interviews as a form of primary research, you will have needed to set up the interview, negotiate the date and time, the duration of the interview and the location. During the interview itself you will have needed to lead the process, and prompt and encourage responses from your participants. You may also have needed to explain your questions more fully.

Phone calls

It is likely that you will have had to make formal phones calls during your research project. These may have been to set up your interview, or to identify whom you needed to write to in order to obtain permission to carry out a survey. You may also have telephoned organisations for information.

Discussion

Discussion will have taken place as you explained the basis of your research and its outline to your tutor in the initial stages. Further on in the research process, you will have needed to describe and explain the main focus of your work to your participants (or alternatively, to the 'gatekeepers' for the participants), making sure that they understood what you were asking from them and also the extent of any involvement.

Within your tutor group you are likely to have been asked to discuss research methods and carry out activities to consolidate your learning. These would also have included discussion.

WRITTEN SKILLS

Having reached the research element of your course of study, you should already have well-established written skills. However, your research may have necessitated forms of written communication which were unfamiliar to you. Examples of this would include:

- contacting organisations
- writing questionnaires
- writing aims and objectives.

Contacting organisations

Writing formal letters is a skill. If you showed your letters to your tutor at the draft stage, any ambiguities or problems with style, content or formality will have been addressed.

Writing questionnaires

Writing questionnaires is, as discussed earlier in this book, not as easy as it may look. If you have used questionnaires as a form of primary research you will have planned, piloted and reviewed the layout and structure of your questionnaires. If you have included interviews in your research process you will have needed to write questions to suit the structure of your interview. Writing for both of these methods is a skill.

Writing aims and objectives

One of the first aspects of your project will have been to set out what you are aiming to achieve. You will have needed to set out these aims and objectives clearly and precisely. Again this will have been a new experience for many students, encouraging a focused approach to your project, and defining boundaries.

INFORMATION TECHNOLOGY SKILLS

The use of information technology will have enabled you to give evidence of your established skills and to develop them, as appropriate, through the use of computerised graphs and tables. You will probably have:

- word processed your written presentation materials
- word processed materials to support your oral presentation
- produced graphs, charts and tables through a computer database.

Word processing written presentation materials
Most programmes of study will ask for the written presentation of a piece of research to be word processed. In such programmes students will often be given a grade for their information technology skills or for their key skills.

Word processing materials to support your oral presentation
As discussed in Chapter 9, all resources used during a presentation need to be clear and easily read. Many students will have elected to word process OHP transparencies and handouts.

Producing graphs, charts and tables through a computer database
The use of databases to present numerical data in a visual form will usually be required. Again, this is likely to form part of your general course assessment, and part of a subsequent grade in information technology or the relevant key skills.

NUMERICAL SKILLS

Numerical skills will have been used during your primary research, particularly if you have taken a quantitative approach. The collation and analysis of data will have given evidence of your numerical skills, as will the presentation of your results.

There are a number of statistics packages available and you may have had access to these through your college or school library. These will have offered you additional opportunities for the presentation of numerical data.

Evaluating your own learning

You can evaluate your learning within three useful categories:

- personal development
- academic achievements
- practical skills.

Within each of these you will have been gathering evidence, not only in the areas discussed above, but also to support the three general key skills areas (working with others, improving own learning and performance, and problem solving).

PERSONAL DEVELOPMENT

Areas of personal development would include:

- increased confidence and self-esteem
- negotiating dates and times of interviews
- managing time and action plans
- trying out new approaches to learning and working
- relating to and cooperating and interacting with others
- supporting others through the sharing of resources
- supporting others during discussion and oral presentations
- communicating information both orally and in writing
- treating others with respect
- trying out new ideas
- accepting criticism and general feedback
- supporting others.

Let us consider some of these.

Confidence and self-esteem

Think about how you felt when arranging interviews or access to participants for a survey.

- Were you nervous?
- Did you gain in confidence as your project progressed?
- How did others respond to you?
- Did the comments and cooperation of others make you feel good about what you were doing?
- Are you proud of what you have achieved?

Relating to and interacting with others

- In what ways did you need to interact with other people in order to carry out your research?
- Did you need to interact with people you had not met before?
- How easy or difficult did you find this?
- Did you gain in confidence as your project progressed?

Communicating information both orally and in writing

- What new methods of written communication did you use during your research project?
- What about oral communication?
- Have you grown in confidence with regard to communicating with other people?

Treating others with respect

- Were you always polite and considerate?
- Were you patient?
- Did you give people the time they needed?
- How easy did you find it to identify the ethical issues within your research project?

- Do you consider that you managed to respect the participants in your research project?

Trying out new ideas
- How many new experiences did you sample during your research project?
- How did you feel about them beforehand?
- How did you feel afterwards?
- Would you be prepared to carry them out again another time?

Supporting others
- Were you able to share resources and ideas with others?
- Did you have opportunities to give guidance to others regarding resources or ideas?
- Did you listen to and respect the views of others during discussion?
- Did you respect and support your peers during their oral presentations?
- How well did you accept criticism and general feedback from your tutor?
- How well did you accept criticism and general feedback from your peers?

ACADEMIC ACHIEVEMENTS

Academic achievement would include:
- the overall success of the project
- meeting targets
- use of a variety of information sources
- receiving and responding to a variety of information
- dealing with complex data
- problem solving
- applying numeracy.

Let us consider some of these.

The overall success of the project
Refer back to the list of 25 questions at the beginning of this chapter. If you have worked through these you have already considered how successful you think your project has been.

Meeting targets
- How well did you manage your time?
- Did you distribute your questionnaires (if you used them) in plenty of time?
- Did you collect them again promptly?
- Have you fulfilled all the criteria for the research module?

Use of a variety of information sources
- How many different information sources did you incorporate into your research project?
- Were your chosen sources appropriate?
- Were there other sources that (with hindsight) you should also have explored?

Receiving and responding to a variety of information

- How well did you critically evaluate the literature on your topic area?
- Were you able to identify particular strengths within it?
- Were you able to identify any issues of concern within it?
- How easy did you find it to select relevant material for your project?
- How successfully did you collate, evaluate and present the data you received from your primary research?

Dealing with complex data

- How easy or difficult did you find it to calculate and collate numerical data?
- Were you able to understand statistics produced by others, relevant to your research?
- Were you able to understand the statistics presented by your peers during their oral presentations?
- Did you understand your own numerical data?
- Were you able to explain your numerical data clearly?
- Has your ability to interpret and explain data improved during this piece of research?

Problem solving

Most research projects have a 'hiccup' at some point. This might involve needing to rearrange interviews at the last minute, or having difficulties in getting questionnaires returned.

- What problems did you need to overcome?
- How well do you think you coped with them?
- How difficult was it to reschedule planned events?
- Did this have any lasting effect on your project?

PRACTICAL SKILLS

Practical skills would include:
- carrying out a literature search
- applying creative skills
- using technology
- using audio-visual resources.

Let us consider each of these.

Carrying out a literature search

- How well did you manage when carrying out a literature search?
- How well did you know your way around the library?
- Have you gained a greater knowledge of the library whilst carrying out this project?
- What did you learn from the literature search?

Applying creative skills
- Have you been able to incorporate creativity into your research project?
- In what ways?
- Were any of these new ways for you?

Using technology
- How much have you used technology in the past?
- Do you usually word process your assignment work?
- What forms of technology have you used for the first time during your research project?
- How well do you feel you managed them?
- Do you now feel more confident about using technology? In what ways?

Using audio-visual resources
- Which audio-visual resources (if any) did you use during your oral presentation?
- How well do you feel you managed them?
- What difficulties did you have to overcome?
- Do you now feel more confident about using these resources?

Using your skills

WHERE NEXT?

Having developed and enhanced a variety of skills during the research and presentation process, you now need to evaluate how this new learning can be taken forward into other situations. Hopefully many of your new or enhanced skills will be useful to you in the future, either immediate or longer term:
- in your academic development, as you move into further courses of study
- in the workplace, in your role as a practitioner in your chosen career
- in your life in general.

Activity
Consider how you will be able to transfer the skills which you have identified through the sections above, to what you do or will be doing in future courses of study, in the practical setting of your future career, or in your life in general. Use Figures 10.1 to 10.4, which you may photocopy, to make a note of your answers under the different headings or questions.

Evaluating the research process and outcomes

1 Were your aims and objectives clear?

2 Were they fully met?
3 If not, can you identify why this was the case?

4 If you set a hypothesis, was it proved or disproved?
5 If you set yourself a research question, was it answered?

6 Were the parameters you set yourself appropriate? How do you justify this?

7 How successful was your primary research?
8 Would an alternative method have been better?

9 How well did you interact with participants involved with your primary research?

10 How many new experiences did you have in carrying out and presenting your work?

11 Was your literature base sufficient for the scope of your project?

12 Did you identify all the ethical issues that you should have?

13 How well did you present your data?

This page may be photocopied.   © Stanley Thornes (Publishers) Ltd

14 How well did you discuss it? Were you analytical, or simply descriptive? 15 Were you able to draw conclusions?
16 How reliable do you consider your outcomes to be? How can you justify this?
17 What technology did you use during your research? What aspect of this was new to you?
18 Does your work meet the module requirements?
19 How good is the written presentation of your work? Could it have been improved? 20 How well written is your work? Did you check your spellings and grammar?
21 Is your work set out in a logical order?
22 How well does your work flow?
23 How well did you manage your time?
24 Does your work reflect the length of time allocated to complete it?
25 Do you think your work has earned you a pass grade? Or higher? Why?

This page may be photocopied.

Figure 10.1   Evaluating the research process and outcomes

How have your skills developed in the following areas?
Oral skills
Written skills
Information technology skills
Numerical skills

This page may be photocopied.   © Stanley Thornes (Publishers) Ltd.

Figure 10.2   Evaluating skills development

How have you developed in the following areas?

Personal development

Academic achievements

Practical skills

This page may be photocopied.   © *Stanley Thornes (Publishers) Ltd.*

Figure 10.3   Evaluating other areas of development

How will you apply your new or enhanced skills to the following?

In further academic development

To the workplace

To your life in general

This page may be photocopied.

Figure 10.4   Using your skills

Chapter summary

■ Evaluation is an important skill.
■ Evaluation includes planning, actions and different forms of presentation.
■ The research process encourages skills that can be applied to others areas.
■ Personal development is promoted during the research process.
■ Academic achievement is demonstrated through the outcomes of the research process.
■ Practical skills are enhanced during the research process.

GLOSSARY OF TERMS

Abstract
An abstract is a brief summary of the whole project. It states the aims, the research methods used, and the conclusions drawn. This gives an 'at a glance' summary of your work.

Action research
The type of research used when a researcher wants to study their own working environment, for example, teachers wanting to find out more specific information about how their classroom functions. Action implies the intention to change practice following the outcomes of the study.

Aim
In the context of a research proposal, 'aim' refers to the overall purpose.

Ambiguity
This is a statement or word which can have more than one meaning.

Anecdote
A short example of something – often funny – used to illustrate a point.

Anonymity
Not being identified, having no known name or individual features.

Appendix
An 'add on' or a separate supplement of additional material to your work, referred to in your writing.

Audio-visual resources
Relating to sound or visual resources, such as video or audio tapes. Can form part of both primary and secondary research. Can also be used during an oral presentation.

Bar chart
Bar charts are a popular choice of method for presenting simple data. They are easy to draw and, if done correctly, easy to understand. They are most appropriate for presenting data or 'quantities' for descriptive categories (e.g. the number of people using different forms of transport to reach their local nursery), or data for discrete quantities (how many children are one, two, three or four years old in a nursery).

Bias
Showing a preference or inclination towards something or someone.

Bibliography
Most books include a bibliography, usually found at the end. This sets out a range of publications relevant to the main subjects covered by the book itself.

Case study
A study of a situation, for example a group or a family, where the researcher looks at a range of factors relevant to what they are studying.

Category response
A type of answer often used on questionnaires. At times it is necessary to place answers into categories. An example of a category response question could be:
How long ago did you qualify?
0–3 years ___ 4–8 years ___ 9–12 years ___ 13–16 years ___ other ___

CD-ROM
A system of information storage held on compact disk. Libraries often hold a range of CD-ROMs for use on library computers.

Chronological
Setting information out in a specific sequence, for example, in date order.

Cited
Quoted or referred to within a written passage.

Closed question
A question which has a specific answer, often yes or no. The opposite of an open question.

Collate
Grouping material together from different sources to produce a set of data.

Confidentiality
Keeping information to oneself, normally when it has been entrusted by someone else. This information may be written or spoken.

Continuum
A continuous imaginary line upon which responses/opinions can be placed.

Copyright
Having the exclusive right to use material.

Covert
In secret. An act or observation carried out without the permission or knowledge of the person(s) involved.

Cross-cultural research
Research which focuses on a range of cultures, either within a single community or across a range of communities.

Cross-sectional research
Research which takes a 'slice' (a cross-section) of its target group and bases its overall findings on the views or behaviours of those targeted, assuming them to be typical of the whole group.

Dewey decimal system
Libraries have their contents divided up into logical categories. The most commonly used system for classifying this is the **Dewey decimal system**, which divides subjects both by type and by number. Books in libraries have both broad subject areas and smaller subject divisions.

Direct participant observation
Observation whereby researchers obtain their findings by having joined in with the situation they are observing.

ERIC
Educational Resources Information Centre
ERIC can usually be found in the academic libraries of higher education. It is less likely to be available in other libraries. It is a facility which searches for information from the key words it has been given, producing titles of books and details of articles. It does not actually give you the information you are looking for, just suitable sources for further research, in the form of book titles.

Et al.
'and others'. A term used in referencing, when quoting from work produced by more than three authors.

Ethics
Moral values held by an individual or a group. The study of ethics involves consideration of the principles that govern human conduct.

Ethnographic
An ethnographic study is one whereby the researcher lives for a period of time within a particular community in order to find out more about their cultural ways and values.

Footnotes
Notes at the bottom of a page of text (a referencing method).

Gatekeeper
If you are intending to carry out your research in a school or similarly large establishment, the headteacher or management team (often referred to as the 'gatekeepers' because they give you access to where you want to be) need to give

their written consent. They are held *in loco parentis* (in the place of a parent) whilst children are in their care. This permission needs to be arranged well in advance, so again your time management and planning is important. The 'gatekeepers' will usually require full details of what you intend to do.

Harvard system
The commonly used system for referencing and writing a bibliography. Usually required by further education and higher education institutions.

Hypothesis
A statement which the researcher sets out to either prove or disprove. It may be single-ended or open-ended.

Interview
Interviews are useful for both quantitative and qualitative research, depending on the questions asked. Interviews can be either structured or unstructured, and can also be a mixture of both. Interviews are particularly useful if you are trying to find out people's individual opinions or experiences.

Invalidate
To remove value or effectiveness. To render something ineffective.

ISBN
International Standard Book Number. A numerical means of identifying or ordering a particular publication.

Line graph
Line graphs are good at showing trends or changes in quantities, especially over time. They are used where the horizontal axis represents a continuously variable quantity such as age, time or temperature. The line of such a graph is formed by joining a series of discrete points plotted from the raw data collected.

Literature base
A selection of relevant published material to support research, gathered together by the researcher. A form of secondary research.

Longitudinal research
A study carried out over a considerable period of time, for example, a study of development.

Mean
The mean is the score which we usually recognise as being the average. We calculate it by summing all the scores we are dealing with and then dividing the total by the number of those scores.

Median

The median is the point in the 'row' or 'sequence' that divides the lower half from the higher half. The central point of a range of number 'scores'.

Methodology

A system of approaches or methods taken towards achieving an aim.

Microfiche

An information storage system on postcard-sized sheets of film which can be enlarged and read on an appropriate viewer.

Mode

The mode is the score that is the most common in a set of data. The most commonly found 'score' in a range of numbers.

Non-direct participant observation

Observing from a distance/without involvement, therefore having no impact on what is happening.

Objectives

A breakdown of our aim, noting specific smaller steps to achieving our overall aim.

Objectivity

An impartial viewpoint. Taking a fair and open-minded approach to something.

Observation

An important and useful option for researchers which allows you to see what is really happening. It is, however, not easy and would not normally be favoured by inexperienced researchers. Observation is useful because, whereas when you are carrying out an interview your participant may tell you that they consider X to be their preferred option, during observation you may see that in practice they really follow Y instead. In this respect observation can obtain a truer overall result.

Open question

A question which encourages unrestricted answers. They cannot usually be answered with yes or no.

Parameters

Setting parameters means deciding how broad or narrow your study will be. Parameters are boundaries.

Paraphrasing

The rewording of material written by others.

Pictograph

A pictograph is a way of drawing a chart in symbolic or pictorial style, but serves a similar purpose to a bar chart. Small pictures or symbols are used to represent given quantities, and the resultant chart is divided into rows or columns.

Pie chart

A circular chart, resembling a pie divided into slices of varying size which represent particular quantities of the various categories measured or surveyed.

Piloting

A trial run, prior to the main event. Piloting means asking a small number of 'similar' participants to, for example, complete your questionnaire and comment on the layout, the instructions for completion of the questionnaire, and the clarity of your questions. You will also be able to find out how long your questionnaire takes to answer. Sometimes the meaning of questions can seem obvious to you, the writer, but is far from clear to others reading them. The piloting process helps get rid of any ambiguities.

Plagiarism

Using material belonging to others, without an acknowledgement. It is looked upon seriously by all colleges and universities.

Primary data

Information gathered by the researcher themselves. New data.

Primary research

An enquiry that you have carried out yourself in order to obtain data not gathered by anyone else before you, in the same situation.

Qualitative research

Research which obtains viewpoints and personal feelings from its participants.

Quantitative research

Research which produces results which can be expressed using numbers or statistics and set out in graphs, tables or charts.

Questionnaire

A form of primary resarch. There are many points for consideration when planning a questionnaire. It can often seem the easiest method of gathering primary data, but questionnaires are not as easy to produce as they may look.

Range

The range is the difference between the lowest and the highest result taken from your research.

Ranked response
A classification of responses, often used in questionnaires, whereby the participant places their answers in order of importance.

Raw data
Information gathered from research, before collation. Raw data are the information you receive on your questionnaires, in your interview notes, your observation notes, and so on. Your raw data are not usually seen by anyone other than you (and your tutor).

Referencing
The acknowledgement of a source of information in your text. Making an accurate and formal note of each source referred to in your writing.

Reliability
Reliability is similar to validity but in research terms refers more to the method by which we gather our information. It relies on our having used an appropriate research method.

Replication
Something which will be the same when repeated again. Successful replication of a method of research more than once is the only way to demonstrate reliability.

Scaled response
A classification of responses, often used in questionnaires, e.g. 'Strongly agree, Agree, Disagree, Strongly disagree'.

Scattergram
A graphical method of showing links between data.

Search engine
Search engines are programs set up to guide you easily through a mass of information on the Internet, to what is relevant to you. Examples of popular search engines are *Yahoo!* and *Ask Jeeves*.

Secondary data
Information collated and presented by someone else which you have chosen to use to support your work.

Secondary research
The use of material researched and/or written by others which you have identified as useful to your own research.

Sociogram
Sociograms represent data that describe the relationships between different members of a social group. They can be used to depict the social relationships of just

one member of the group, or they can be used to show patterns of relationships within the whole group.

Standard deviation
Sometimes the range of numerical data can be shown on a chart as the standard deviation. This gives a curved illustration of all the 'scores' gathered. Showing variations in data, from a specific point.

Statistics
A collection and classification of data often produced during primary research, and also used as secondary research by others.

Subjectivity
A viewpoint influenced by one's own opinion. Excessive subjectivity could mean being unable to take an open-minded position.

Table
The most basic way of presenting numerical or written information.

Target group
A specific group of people needed for focus or involvement, relevant to what they are being asked to do or comment on.

Transcribe
To write down what has been recorded on audio tape following an interview.

Triangulation
The supporting of research findings by several methods, for example, the findings from observation together with the outcomes of a survey and statistics from past research.

Validity
Something is valid if we know that it is true; that it is accurate; that it measures what it is claiming to measure. If it is valid it is unlikely to be disputed. In research terms, validity is described as something which actually gives a true representation of what was being researched.

Venn diagram
A Venn diagram shows how different sets of data can be free-standing and can also partially overlap. The common ground (or overlap) is shown by the area of each part of the circles which are linked.

Web site
An Internet site where information can be located.

RELEVANT JOURNALS AND MAGAZINES

Art and Craft (Monthly)	Scholastic Ltd	Articles by practising teachers
Care standard (10 issues a year)	In House	Covers training in care settings
Child Abuse Review (5 issues a year)	John Wiley & Sons Ltd	Covers practice development, research findings, training initiatives, policy issues
Child and Family Law Quarterly (Quarterly)	Jordan Publishing Ltd	Covers major legislation and judicial developments
Child Psychology and Psychiatry Review (Quarterly)	Cambridge University Press	Articles and reviews relevant to those working in the profession
Childhood (Quarterly)	Saga Publications	Covers a broad range of research relating to children
Childminding (Quarterly)	Scottish Childminding Association	Covers all aspects of childminding and childcare
Children in the News (Weekly)	National Children's Bureau	A selection of relevant media articles from the previous week
Children's Social and Economics Education (3 issues a year)	Multilingual Matters Ltd	Covers variety of disciplines relating education to economics, sociology, etc.
Child Education (Monthly)	Scholastic Ltd	Pre-school and early years education
Childright (10 issues a year)	The Children's Legal Centre Ltd	Bulletin of law and policy affecting young people
Children First (3 issues a year)	UNICEF UK	Children's news in UK and developing countries
Children in Focus (3 issues a year)	The Children's Society	The magazine of the Society
Childrens Literature Review (Quarterly)	Gale Research	Covers current issues
Co-ordinate (Monthly)	National Early Years Network	Up-to-date issues in early years care
Community Care (Weekly)	Reed Business Publishing	Topics for anyone working in social care
Connect Bulletin on Learning Difficulties (Quarterly)	Connect	For people with learning difficulties and their support network
Counselling (Quarterly)	British Association for Counselling	Journal of the Association
Counselling at Work (Quarterly)	Public Association of Counselling at Work	Articles particularly relevant to practising counsellors
Early Years – Journal of TACTYC (Quarterly)	Trentham Books	A journal of research and development
Early Childhood Practice (2 issues a year)	Early Childhood Practice	A journal for multi-professional partnerships
Early Development and Parenting (Quarterly)	John Wiley & Sons Ltd	Reviews and reports of psychological developments
Family Policy Bulletin (Quarterly)	Family Policy Studies Centre	News and advice on family-related issues

Focus (Quarterly)	Carlton Hill Publishers	A newsletter for staff working with people with visual and learning difficulties
Health and Safety at work (Monthly)	Butterworths Tolley	Journal of the working environment
Health Education (Quarterly)	Health Education Authority	Issues for health professionals
Health Matters (Quarterly)	Health Matters Publications Ltd	Reports and analyses of the health service and public health issues
Health Which? (Bi-monthly)	Which? Ltd	Guidelines for a healthier life
Infant and Nursery School (3 issues a year)	Woodlands Media Education	Equipment and resources for early years teachers
Infant Projects (Monthly)	Scholastic Ltd	Practical project ideas for use in the classroom
Junior Education (Monthly)	Scholastic Ltd	Up-to-date education news
Literacy and Learning (Bi-monthly)	Questions Publishing Co Ltd	The literacy curriculum
New Statesman (Weekly)	New Statesman Ltd	News and current affairs
Nursery World (Weekly)	Times Supplements Ltd	Early years education and care
Nursery Projects (Monthly)	Scholastic Ltd	Includes focused projects for use with the under-fives
Nursing Ethics (Bi-monthly)	Arnold	Journal for healthcare professionals
Nursing Home Business (10 issues a year)	Part View Publishing Ltd	Running and organisation of nursing homes
Nursing Times (Weekly)	EMAP Healthcare	Various aspects of nursing
Practical Pre-school	Step Forward Publishing Ltd	Practical help and guidance in pre-school settings
Primary Maths and Science (9 issues a year)	The Questions Publishing Co	Practical ideas and articles on the National Curriculum
Psychology Review (Monthly)	Philip Allen Updates	Articles on a range of psychology topics, popular with A-level students
Residential Care Products (Quarterly)	AJP Publishing	Articles and discussion of products relating to the care sector
Special Children (9 issues a year)	Questions Publishing Co Ltd	Special educational needs of children with learning difficulites
TES Primary (Monthly)	Times Newspapers Ltd	Supplement on all matters relating to primary education, within the Times Educational Supplement
The Psychologist (Monthly)	The British Psychological Society	Bulletin of the Society
The Skill Journal (Monthly)	National Bureau for Students with Disabilities	Education, training and employment for people with learning difficulties and/or disabilities

SUGGESTED INFORMATION SOURCES

Public libraries
A useful starting point. Many have their own on-line catalogue

School libraries
A range of relevant topic areas will be found

Further education college libraries
A range of publications relevant to all the courses offered, together with a range of general information and information technology sources

Higher education libraries
As further education colleges, together with more specific information technology sources for research purposes

Information bureaus
Local information covering the area in which it is based

Bookshops
Bookshops will order copies of publications especially for you. Delivery usually takes around three weeks

Publishers
Educational publishers have lists and promotional material which may help you find additional material for your field of study; many publishers now have their own web-sites

Citizens Advice Bureau
An ideal place to obtain local community information and advice

Databases
A range of databases can be found in libraries. Organisations also have information and statistics stored on databases which you may be able to access indirectly through their staff

Writing to subject specific organisations, such as Kidsclub Network
Some organisations will be directly relevant to your research subject. Writing to them directly will often enable you to obtain up-to-date information as well as information about other useful sources

Writing to charities (e.g. the NSPCC)
Charities are excellent sources of information, but remember that it is important that you send a large stamped addressed envelope to ensure no cost is incurred by them. Whenever possible, try to send a donation to the charity too

Government offices (such as DfEE)
These are of particular use if you are researching an issue of current educational importance

Health centres and GP surgeries
Most communities have a health centre. Your own GP surgery will also usually have information material on a wide variety of health and family issues

Education award bodies
Award bodies for courses may be able to help you particularly if your subject involves historical perspectives of a subject area

British agencies
Aid agencies, relief agencies, adoption agencies and so on can be good sources of up-to-date information

Foreign embassies in Britain
If the scope of your research includes, for example, researching statistics, life styles or education in another country, the embassy for that country can usually be found in London

Government offices
Government offices are usually very willing to send information discussed during sessions in the House of Commons and House of Lords, recorded in Hansard. They are also good sources of other information on current parliamentary issues

Telephone information lines
It is important that you never call *help* lines such as Childline. Examples of telephone *information* lines include: Actionaid Education (01460 238000), The Hearing Research Trust (020 7833 1733) and Hyperactive Children's support Group (01903 725182)

Equal Opportunities Commission
This is an excellent source of information relevant to all issues of equality and legislation

The National Society for Religious Education
A relevant source of material for education guidelines and associated material

Early Years networks
All local authorities now have early years networks. These include EYCDPs (Early Years Development and Childcare Partnerships). They have general information on childcare and education issues in the authority, together with statistics about relevant provision for young children

REFERENCES AND FURTHER READING

Abbott, L. and Moylett, H. (1997a) *Working with the under-3s: Responding to Children's Needs* (Buckingham, Open University Press)

Abbott, L. and Moylett, H. (1997b) *Working with the under-3s: Training and Professional Development* (Buckingham, Open University Press)

Barnes, P. (1995) *Personal, Social and Emotional Development of Children* (Oxford, Open University Press)

Bee, H. (1992) *The Developing Child*, 6th edition (New York, HarperCollins)

Bell, J. (1999) *Doing Your Research Project*, 3rd edition (Buckingham, Open University Press; first published 1987)

Cemlyn, S. (1999) 'On the road to understanding', *Community Care*, no. 1285, 12 August, pp. 24–5

Clarke, L. Sach, B. and Sumner, S. (1995) *GNVQ Advanced Health and Social Care* (Cheltenham, Stanley Thornes)

Cullis, T., Dolan, L. and Groves, D.(1999) *Psychology for You* (Cheltenham, Stanley Thornes)

Dare, A. and O'Donovan, M. (1996) *A Practical Guide to Child Nutrition* (Cheltenham, Stanley Thornes)

Dare, A. and O'Donovan, M. (1998) *Good Practice in Caring for Young Children with Special Needs* (Cheltenham, Stanley Thornes)

Department of Health (1991) *Child Abuse* (London, HMSO)

Elliott, M. (1992) *Protecting Children* (London, HMSO)

Fagot, B. (1978) 'The influence of sex of child on parental reactions to toddler children', cited in Cullis *et al.* (1999)

Hobart, C. and Frankel, J. (1999) *A Practical Guide to Child Observation and Assessment*, 2nd edition (Cheltenham, Stanley Thornes)

Jameson, H. and Watson, M. (1998) *Starting and Running a Nursery* (Cheltenham, Stanley Thornes)

Malik, H. (1998) *A Practical Guide to Equal Opportunities* (Cheltenham, Stanley Thornes)

Moore, S. (1998) *Social Welfare Alive* (Cheltenham, Stanley Thornes)

Oates, J. (1994) *The Foundations of Child Development* (Milton Keynes, Open University Press)

Pollard, A. (1987) *Children and Their Primary Schools* (London, Falmer Press)

Prior, B. (1999) 'Swallowed up by the system', *Community Care*, no. 1283, 29 July, pp. 26–7

Prior, V., Lynch, M. and Glaser, E. (1994) *Messages from Children* (London, NCH Action for Children)

Reder, P., Duncan, S. and Gray, M. (1993) *Beyond Blame* (London, Routledge)

Stoyle, J. (1991) *Caring for Older People* (Cheltenham, Stanley Thornes)

Talay-Ongen, A. (1998) *Typical and Atypical Development in Early Childhood* (Leicester, BPS Books)

Whiting, B. B. and Whiting, J. W. M. (1975) *Children of Six Cultures: A Psycho-Cultural Analysis* (Cambridge, Mass., Harvard University Press)

Yarrow, M. R. and Waxler, C. Z. (1975) 'The emergence and functions of prosocial behaviour in young children', cited in Barnes (1995)

INDEX